DATE DUE

BERENSON'S
ITALIAN PICTURES
OF THE RENAISSANCE

PHAIDON

DUCCIO: *Predella panel from the back of the Maestà: The Calling of the Sons of Zebedee.*
Washington, National Gallery of Art, Kress Collection. *1308–11.*

ITALIAN PICTURES OF THE RENAISSANCE

A LIST OF THE PRINCIPAL ARTISTS
AND THEIR WORKS
WITH AN INDEX OF PLACES

BY

BERNARD BERENSON

CENTRAL ITALIAN AND
NORTH ITALIAN SCHOOLS
IN THREE VOLUMES

VOLUME II

PLATES 1–994

PHAIDON

LISTS OF WORKS BY ITALIAN RENAISSANCE PAINTERS FIRST PUBLISHED IN
1897 (CENTRAL ITALIAN PAINTERS) AND 1907 (NORTH ITALIAN PAINTERS)
REVISED EDITION 1932

NEWLY REVISED AND ILLUSTRATED 1968
ADDITIONAL AND REVISED MATERIAL © PHAIDON PRESS LTD · LONDON · 1968

PHAIDON PUBLISHERS INC · NEW YORK
DISTRIBUTORS IN THE UNITED STATES: FREDERICK A. PRAEGER INC
111 FOURTH AVENUE · NEW YORK · N.Y. 10003
LIBRARY OF CONGRESS CATALOG CARD NUMBER: 68-18905

SBN for complete set of three volumes: 7148 1324 9
SBN for this volume: 7148 1355 9

MADE IN GREAT BRITAIN
TEXT PRINTED BY R. & R. CLARK LTD · EDINBURGH
ILLUSTRATIONS PRINTED BY LONSDALE & BARTHOLOMEW LTD · LEICESTER

CENTRAL ITALIAN AND NORTH ITALIAN
PICTURES OF THE RENAISSANCE

ACKNOWLEDGEMENTS

Paintings in the Royal Collection are reproduced by gracious permission of Her Majesty The Queen.

Gratitude is due to all private owners who have given permission for their paintings to be reproduced and in many cases have provided new photographs. Grateful acknowledgement is also made to the authorities of numerous museums and institutions for providing photographs and information and for permission to reproduce pictures in their collections.

CORRIGENDA

The locations given in the following captions should be amended as follows:

Plate 82 (Pietro Lorenzetti): Siena, Pinacoteca.

Plates 163-164 (Cavallini Follower): St.-Jean-Cap-Ferrat, Musée Ile-de-France.

Plate 285 (Lippo Dalmasio): Norton Hall, Sir Walter Pollen.

Plate 320 (Ceccarelli): Formerly Richmond, Cook Collection.

Plate 847 (Benvenuto di Giovanni): Formerly Capesthorne Hall, Sir Walter Bromley Davenport.

Plate 888 (Francesco di Giorgio): Siena, Pinacoteca.

Plate 1149 (Balducci): Compton Wynyates, Marquess of Northampton.

Plate 1362 (Zenale): Isolabella, Borromeo Collection.

Plates 708, 709 (Mantegna): Delete "Cartoon for lost frescoes".

PLATES

THE ROMANESQUE AND
EARLY GOTHIC PERIODS

1. BERLINGHIERI: *Painted Crucifix*. Lucca, Pinacoteca. *Signed*.

2. BONAVENTURA BERLINGHIERI: *S. Francis and scenes from his life*. Pescia, S. Francesco.
Signed and dated 1235.

3. MASTER OF ST. FRANCIS: *S. Francis between two Angels*. Assisi, S. Maria degli Angeli.

4. MASTER OF ST. FRANCIS: *Entombment*. Perugia, Galleria Nazionale.

5. MASTER OF ST. FRANCIS: *Fresco: S. Francis receiving stigmata*. Detail. Assisi, S. Francesco, Lower Church.

6. GIUNTA PISANO: *The dead Christ in the Tomb*. Brussels, Stoclet Collection.

7. GIUNTA PISANO: *Painted Crucifix*. Bologna, S. Domenico. *Signed*.

8. MARGARITO: *S. Francis* Ganghereto, Parish Church. *Signed.*

9. MARGARITO: *Madonna and Child.* Washington, National Gallery of Art, Kress Collection. *Signed.*

10. MARGARITO: *S. Francis.* Zürich, Kunsthaus. *Signed.*

11–12. MARGARITO: *Details of dossal: S. John Evangelist in the cauldron of boiling oil; S. Margaret unharmed by the dragon.* London, National Gallery. *Signed.*

13. MARGARITO: *Detail of dossal: Madonna and Child.* London, National Gallery. *Signed.*

14. DEODATO ORLANDI: *Painted Crucifix*. Lucca, Pinacoteca. *Signed and dated 1288.*

15. Deodato Orlandi: *Dossal: Madonna and Child with Saints and Angels.* Detail. Pisa, Museo Nazionale. *Signed and dated 1301.*

16. Deodato Orlandi: *Visitation, Birth of the Baptist, Naming of the Baptist, the Baptist preaching.* Berlin-Dahlem, Staatliche Museen.

17. MASTER OF THE BAPTIST'S DOSSAL: *S. John Baptist enthroned and twelve scenes from his life*. Detail.
Siena, Pinacoteca.

18. GUIDO DA SIENA: *St. Clare repulsing the Saracens with a pyx*. Detail of reliquary shutter. Siena, Pinacoteca.

19. GUIDO DA SIENA: *Dossal: Madonna and Child with SS. Francis, John Baptist, John Evangelist and Mary Magdalen.* Siena, Pinacoteca. *Dated 1271.*

20. GUIDO DA SIENA: *Nativity.* Paris, Stroelin Collection.

21. GUIDO DA SIENA: *Centre panel of S. Domenico altarpiece: Madonna and Child enthroned.*
Siena, Palazzo Pubblico. *Signed and dated 1221 (originally dated 1261 or 1271 or 1281?).*

22. GUIDO DA SIENA: *Detail of a Lenten hanging: Christ's Entry into Jerusalem*. Siena, Pinacoteca.

23. VIGOROSO DA SIENA: *Detail of dossal: S. Juliana*. Perugia, Galleria Nazionale. *Signed and dated 128(o?)*.

24–5. MEO DA SIENA: *Dossal: Christ enthroned with Saints; Madonna and Child enthroned with Saints*. Details. Frankfurt, Staedel Institute. *Dated 1333*.

26–7. MEO DA SIENA: *Dossal: Madonna and Child enthroned with Saints*. Details of left half. Frankfurt, Staedel Institute. *Dated 1333*.

28. MEO DA SIENA: *Polyptych: Madonna and Child with Saints*. Detail. Perugia, Galleria Nazionale. *Signed*.

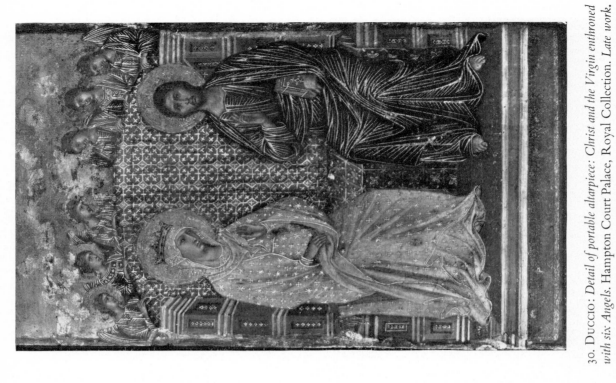

30. DUCCIO: *Detail of portable altarpiece: Christ and the Virgin enthroned with six Angels. Hampton Court Palace, Royal Collection. Late work.*

29. DUCCIO: *Madonna and Child enthroned with four Angels and three Franciscan monks. Siena, Pinacoteca. Early work.*

32. DUCCIO: *Detail from front of the Maestà: S. Catherine. Siena, Opera del Duomo. Signed. 1308–11.*

31. DUCCIO: *Detail of portable altarpiece: Madonna and Child. London, National Gallery.*

33. DUCCIO and assistant: *Portable altar-piece: Crucifixion with blessing Redeemer and two Angels above;
in wings, two Bishop Saints.* Boston, Museum of Fine Arts.

34. DUCCIO: *Predella panel from the front of the Maestà: Isaiah, Nativity, Ezekiel.* Washington,
National Gallery of Art, Mellon Collection, *1308–11*.

35. Detail from plate 33.

36. DUCCIO: *Predella panel from the back of the Maestà: Temptation of Christ.*
New York, Frick Collection. *1308–11.*

37. DUCCIO: *Detail from the front of the Maestà: The Virgin receives the annunciation of her imminent death.*
Siena, Opera del Duomo. *1308–11.*

38. DUCCIO: *Crucifixion*. Balcarres, Earl of Crawford and Balcarres.

39. CLOSE IMITATOR OF DUCCIO (Master of Badia a Isola): *Madonna and Child enthroned with two Angels.*
Badia a Isola, SS. Salvatore e Cirino.

40. UGOLINO DI NERIO: *Predella panel from S. Croce polyptych: Flagellation*. Berlin-Dahlem, Staatliche Museen.

41. UGOLINO DI NERIO: *Predella panel from S. Croce polyptych: Last Supper*. New York, Robert Lehman.

42. UGOLINO DI NERIO: *S. Michael slaying the dragon*. Grosseto, Museo d'Arte Sacra.

43. UGOLINO DI NERIO: *Madonna and Child enthroned with donor*. San Casciano, S. Maria della Misericordia.

44. UGOLINO DI NERIO: *Fragmentary polyptych: Madonna and Child, SS. Peter and Paul; in pinnacles: Redeemer and two Saints*. Florence, Contini Bonacossi Collection.

45–6. UGOLINO DI NERIO: *Details of polyptych: S. Andrew; S. Stephen.*
Williamstown, Mass., Clark Art Institute. *After 1317.*

47. SEGNA DI BONAVENTURA: *Madonna and Child enthroned with six Angels, SS. John Baptist and Gregory* (?)
and four donors. Castiglione Fiorentino, Collegiata di S. Giuliano. *Signed*.

48. SEGNA DI BONAVENTURA: *Fragmentary polyptych: Madonna and Child, S. Sylvester Gozzolini and S. Benedict.*
New York, Metropolitan Museum. *Signed. Late work.*

49. SEGNA DI BONAVENTURA: *Busts of three Saints.* Homeless.

50. Niccolò di Segna: *Madonna of Mercy*. Vertine, Parish Church. *About 1331*.

51. NICCOLÒ DI SEGNA: *Fresco: S. Fina's vision of S. Gregory announcing her imminent death.*
S. Gimignano, Collegiata.

52. NICCOLÒ DI SEGNA: *Centre panel of polyptych:*
Madonna and Child eating cherries.
Montalcino, Museo Diocesano. *Dated 1346.*

53. NICCOLÒ DI SEGNA: *Madonna and Child.*
Venice, Conte Vittorio Cini.

54. Niccolò di Segna: *Crucifix*. Siena, Pinacoteca. *Signed and dated 1345.*

MASTER OF CITTÀ DI CASTELLO:
55. *Side-panel of polyptych: S. John Baptist.* New Haven, Conn., Yale University Art Gallery.
56. *Centre panel of polyptych: Madonna and Child.* Copenhagen, Royal Museum.

MASTER OF CITTÀ DI CASTELLO:
57. *Fragment of polyptych from Crevole: Madonna and Child.* Siena, Opera del Duomo.
58. *Panel of polyptych: S. Mary Magdalen.* Siena, Pinacoteca.

59. MASTER OF CITTÀ DI CASTELLO: *Madonna and Child enthroned with six Angels and donor.*
Città di Castello, Pinacoteca.

60. CLOSE IMITATOR OF DUCCIO: *Fragment of portable altarpiece:*
Madonna and Child enthroned with four Angels and two Saints.
Homeless.

61. CLOSE IMITATOR OF DUCCIO: *Left half of double diptych: Madonna and Child, Crucifixion.*
Venice, Conte Vittorio Cini.

62. CLOSE IMITATOR OF DUCCIO: *Madonna and Child enthroned
with two Angels*. Homeless.

63. CLOSE IMITATOR OF DUCCIO: *Right half of double diptych: Descent from the Cross, Entombment*.
Venice, Conte Vittorio Cini.

64–6. 'UGOLINO LORENZETTI': *Three panels of polyptych: Madonna and Child.* Fogliano, Pieve; *S. Ansanus and S. Galganus.* Siena, Pinacoteca. *Early work.*

67–9. 'UGOLINO LORENZETTI': *Three panels from S. Cerbone polyptych: S. Catherine.* Washington, National Gallery of Art, Kress Collection; *Madonna and Child, S. John Evangelist.* Lucca, Pinacoteca.

70. 'UGOLINO LORENZETTI': *Nativity*. Cambridge, Mass., Fogg Art Museum.

71. 'UGOLINO LORENZETTI': *Detail of polyptych: Madonna and Child holding crown.* Palermo, Chiaramonte Bordonaro Collection.

72. 'UGOLINO LORENZETTI': *Centre panel of polyptych: Madonna and Child.* Fragment. New Haven, Conn., Yale University Art Gallery.

73–4. 'UGOLINO LORENZETTI': *Side-panels of polyptych: SS. Michael and Agatha; SS. Catherine and Bartholomew.* Pisa, Museo Nazionale di S. Matteo.

75. 'UGOLINO LORENZETTI': *Madonna and Child enthroned with four Angels*. Siena, S. Pietro Ovile.
Late work.

76. PIETRO LORENZETTI: *Madonna and Child.*
Castiglione d'Orcia, Pieve. *Early work.*

77. PIETRO LORENZETTI: *Madonna and Child.*
Montichiello, Pieve.

78. PIETRO LORENZETTI: *Three panels of polyptych: SS. Benedict, Catherine and Margaret.*
Florence, Museo Horne.

79. PIETRO LORENZETTI: *Polyptych: Madonna and Child; SS. Donatus, John Evangelist, John Baptist and Matthew with Angels above; upper row: Annunciation and SS. John, Paul, Vincent, Luke, James, James the Less, Marcellinus, Augustine; in pinnacles, Virgin in Glory and four female Saints.* Arezzo, Pieve. *Signed and dated 1320.*

80. PIETRO LORENZETTI: *Frescoes: Christ in Limbo, Deposition, busts of SS. Rufinus, Catherine, Clare, and Margaret; above the altar: Madonna and Child with SS. John Evangelist and Francis.* Assisi, S. Francesco, Lower Church, left transept.

81. PIETRO LORENZETTI: *Fresco: Massacre of the Innocents*. Detail. Siena, S. Maria dei Servi.

82. PIETRO LORENZETTI: *Detail from the Maestà del Martirio: Madonna and Child.* Sant'Ansano in Dofana, Cappellina del Martirio. *Signed and dated 1329.*

83. PIETRO LORENZETTI: *Predella panel from the Maestà del Martirio: S. Albert hands the Carmelite rule to S. Brocardus.* Siena, Pinacoteca. *1329.*

84–5. PIETRO LORENZETTI: *Two reliquary panels: Christ worshipped by a Dominican.* Homeless. *Madonna and Child worshipped by a Dominican.* Florence, Berenson Collection.

86. Pietro Lorenzetti: *S. John Baptist recommends a warrior to the Madonna.*
Fragmentary fresco. Siena, S. Domenico.

87–8. Pietro Lorenzetti: *Two panels of altarpiece: S. John Evangelist invites S. Humilitas to leave Faenza and her arrival at the gates of Florence; S. Humilitas collects bricks for her church of S. Giovanni Evangelista.*
Florence, Uffizi.

89. PIETRO LORENZETTI: *Altarpiece: The Birth of the Virgin*. Siena, Museo dell'Opera del Duomo.
Signed and dated 1342.

90. AMBROGIO LORENZETTI: *Crucifix*. Siena, Pinacoteca.

91. CLOSE TO AMBROGIO AND PIETRO LORENZETTI: *Allegory of Fall and Redemption*. Siena, Pinacoteca.

92. **Ambrogio Lorenzetti**: *Centre panel of triptych: Madonna and Child holding flowers; at the sides, parts of haloes and martyr's palm.* Fragment. Roccalbegna, Parish Church. *Early work.*

93. **AMBROGIO LORENZETTI**: *Fresco: Martyrdom of Franciscans at Ceuta*. Detail. Siena, S. Francesco.

94. AMBROGIO LORENZETTI: *Detail of the Maestà: Fides*. Massa Marittima, Municipio.

95. AMBROGIO LORENZETTI: *Reconstructed triptych from S. Procolo: 'Berenson' Madonna and Child, with Saviour in pinnacle; SS. Nicholas and Proculus, with S. John Evangelist and S. John Baptist in pinnacles. Florence, Uffizi. Formerly signed and dated 1332.*

96. AMBROGIO LORENZETTI: *Circumcision*. Florence, Uffizi. *Dated 1342.*

97. AMBROGIO LORENZETTI: *Detail from fresco of Good Government: Security and hunting party.*
Siena, Palazzo Pubblico. *1338/40.*

98. AMBROGIO LORENZETTI: *Detail from fresco of Good Government: Dance in the city.*
Siena, Palazzo Pubblico. *1338/40.*

99. PALMERUCCI: *Centre of polyptych: Madonna and Child.*
Formerly Vienna, Lanckoronski Collection.

100. PALMERUCCI: *Right panel of polyptych:
Deacon martyr.* Homeless.

101. PALMERUCCI: *Tondo: Madonna and Child.* Formerly Brussels, van Gelder Collection.

102. PALMERUCCI: *Three panels from polyptych: Madonna and Child, S. John Evangelist, S. Catherine.* Florence, formerly Contessa Serristori.

103. PALMERUCCI: *Madonna and Child enthroned with Saints and kneeling donor.* Gubbio, Palazzo dei Consoli.

104. PALMERUCCI: *Predella panel: A deacon Saint being tortured.* Nancy, Musée.

105. MASTER OF THE CODEX OF ST. GEORGE: *Page from illuminated missal: Nativity.*
New York, Pierpont Morgan Library.

106. MASTER OF THE CODEX OF ST. GEORGE: *Detail of page from illuminated missal: Cardinal Stefaneschi in his study.* Rome, S. Pietro.

107. MASTER OF THE CODEX OF ST. GEORGE: *Detail of page from illuminated missal: St. George killing the dragon.* Rome, S. Pietro.

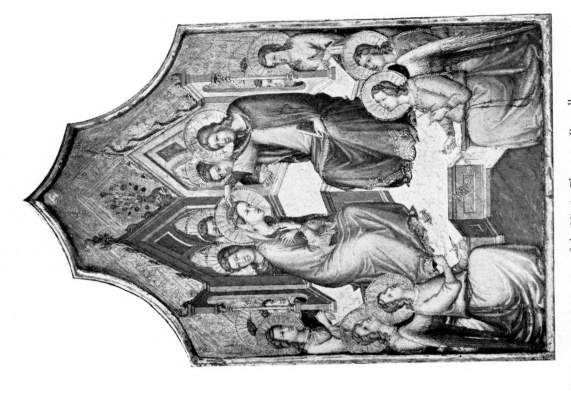

108–9. MASTER OF THE CODEX OF ST. GEORGE: *Diptych: Noli me tangere; Coronation of the Virgin.* Florence, Bargello.

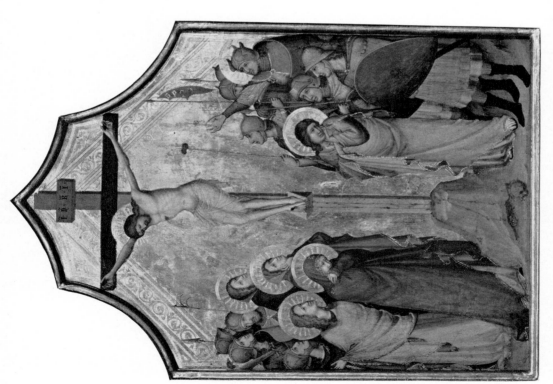

110–11. MASTER OF THE CODEX OF ST. GEORGE: *Diptych: Crucifixion; Entombment.* New York, Metropolitan Museum of Art, Cloisters.

112. MASTER OF THE CODEX OF ST. GEORGE:
SS. Stephen and Lawrence. Detail.
Cracow, Czartoryski Museum.

113. MASTER OF THE CODEX OF ST. GEORGE:
*Reliquary: Madonna and Child enthroned
with SS. John Baptist and John Evangelist.*
Florence, S. Maria del Carmine.

114–15. MASTER OF THE CODEX OF ST. GEORGE: *Angel and Virgin of the Annunciation.* Formerly Brussels,
Mme. Jacques Stoclet.

116. MASTER OF THE CODEX OF ST. GEORGE: *Madonna and Child enthroned
with four Saints and Angels*. Paris, Louvre.

117–18. SIMONE MARTINI: *Side-panels of polyptych: S. Mary Magdalen; S. Augustine.*
MOSCOW, PUSHKIN MUSEUM.

119. SIMONE MARTINI: *Madonna and Child.*
Siena, Pinacoteca.

120. SIMONE MARTINI: *S. John Evangelist mourning.*
Birmingham, Barber Institute.

121. SIMONE MARTINI: *Fresco: Maestà (Madonna and Child enthroned with the four patron Saints of Siena, SS. Savinus, Ansanus, Victor, Crescentius; SS. Peter, Paul, John Evangelist, John Baptist, Catherine, Magdalen, Agnes, Elizabeth of Hungary, the twelve Apostles, Michael, Gabriel, and four other Angels; in the frame: twenty roundels with busts of the Redeemer, Evangelists, Saints and Prophets).* Siena, Palazzo Pubblico, Sala del Mappamondo. *Signed and dated 1315; restored by Simone himself in 1321.*

122. SIMONE MARTINI: *Fresco: S. Martin refuses to take up arms.* Assisi, S. Francesco, Lower Church.

123. SIMONE MARTINI: *Fresco: S. Martin being knighted.* Detail. Assisi, S. Francesco, Lower Church.

124. SIMONE MARTINI: *Detail of polyptych from S. Francesco at Orvieto: Madonna and Child, S. Lucy, S. Catherine; in pinnacles: Christ the Judge and two Angels with the instruments of the Passion.* Boston, Isabella Stewart Gardner Museum.

125–7. SIMONE MARTINI: *Panels of polyptych (from S. Agostino at San Gimignano?): S. Michael.* Cambridge, Fitzwilliam Museum. *Madonna of the goldfinch.* Cologne, Wallraf-Richartz Museum. *S. Catherine.* Homeless.

128. SIMONE MARTINI: *Left panel polyptych from the Jesuit church at Orvieto: S. Catherine with sword.*
Ottawa, National Gallery of Canada.

129. SIMONE MARTINI: *Triptych: Blessed Agostino Novello, four of his miracles, and two Augustinian Saints in roundels*. Siena, S. Agostino.

130. SIMONE MARTINI: *S. Ladislas, king of Hungary*. Altomonte, S. Maria della Consolazione. *Probably 1326.*

131. SIMONE MARTINI: *Christ returning from the Temple*. Liverpool, Walker Art Gallery. *Signed and dated 1342.*

132. SIMONE MARTINI: *Sinopia: Madonna of Humility and Angels.* Avignon, Notre-Dame-des-Doms. *Probably 1341.*

133. SIMONE MARTINI: *Sinopia: Blessing Redeemer.* Avignon, Notre-Dame-des-Doms. *Probably 1341.*

135. SIMONE MARTINI: *Illuminated frontispiece of the Codex Virgilianus.*
Milan, Biblioteca Ambrosiana. 1340–4.

134. SIMONE MARTINI: *Panel from portable altarpiece: Entombment.*
Berlin-Dahlem, Staatliche Museen.

137. MATTEO GIOVANETTI: *Hunting scene.*
Avignon, Palais des Papes, Tour de la Garderobe. *1343–4.*

136. AVIGNONESE FOLLOWER OF SIMONE MARTINI: *Adoration of the Magi.*
New York, Robert Lehman Collection.

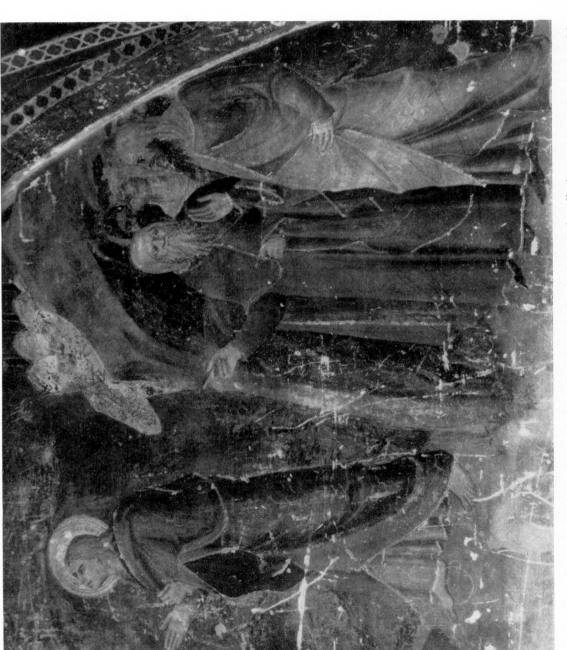

138. MATTEO GIOVANETTI: *Fresco: Crucifixion. Detail. Avignon, Palais des Papes, Chapelle de St. Jean. 1347.*   139. MATTEO GIOVANETTI: *Wing of portable altarpiece: S. Hermagoras with kneeling donor. Venice, Museo Correr.*

141. MATTEO GIOVANETTI: *Fresco: Birth of S. John Baptist. Detail.* Villeneuve-lès-Avignon, Chartreuse. 1355–6.

140. MATTEO GIOVANETTI: *Pendentif frescoes: Prophets. Detail.* Avignon, Palais des Papes, Salle de l'Audience. 1352.

142. MATTEO GIOVANETTI: *Fresco: S. Martial admonishes the kneeling priests at Agen, while two Angels force a demon to destroy a pagan idol.* Avignon, Palais des Papes, Chapelle de S. Martial. *1344–5.*

143. ROBERTO DI ODERISIO: *Fresco: The Sacrament of Matrimony.* Naples, S. Maria Incoronata. *About 1360.*

145. Roberto di Oderisio: *Fresco: The Infant Moses rescued from the Nile. Detail. Naples, S. Maria Incoronata. About 1360.*

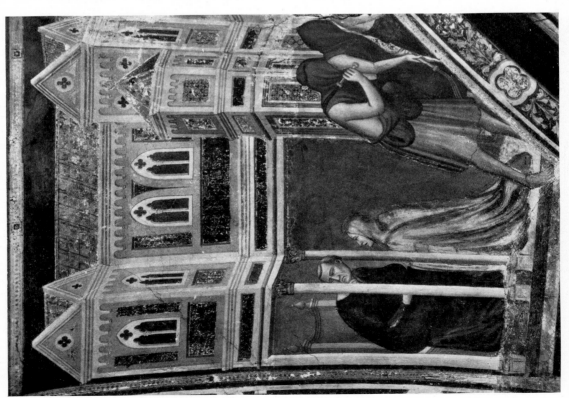

144. Roberto di Oderisio: *Fresco: The Sacrament of Penance. Detail. Naples, S. Maria Incoronata. About 1360.*

147. ROBERTO DI ODERISIO: *Pietà with symbols of the Passion.*
Cambridge, Mass., Fogg Art Museum.

146. ROBERTO DI ODERISIO: *Crucifixion with Franciscan donor.* Detail.
Eboli, S. Francesco. *Signed.*

148. CAVALLINI: *Fresco: Christ in glory and S. George, the Virgin, S. Peter and S. Sebastian.*
Rome, S. Giorgio in Velabro. *Soon after 1295.*

149. CAVALLINI: *Frescoed lunette above the tomb of Cardinal Matteo d'Acquasparta: Madonna and Child with
S. John Evangelist (?), S. Francis and kneeling Cardinal.* Rome, S. Maria in Aracoeli.

150. CAVALLINI: *Detail of fresco of Tree of Jesse: Joachim.* Naples, S. Gennaro.

151. CAVALLINI: *Detail from fresco of Tree of Jesse: The Virgin*. Naples, S. Gennaro.

152. CAVALLINI: *Detail from fresco of Last Judgement: The Virgin*. Rome, S. Cecilia.

153–4. CAVALLINI: *Two details from fresco of Last Judgement: Two Apostles*. Rome, S. Cecilia.

155. CAVALLINI: *Detail from fresco of Last Judgement: Angel*. Rome, S. Cecilia.

156. CAVALLINI: *Mosaic: Annunciation*. Rome, S. Maria in Trastevere.

157–8. ASSISTANT OF CAVALLINI: *Details from fresco of Last Judgement: Angels, Prophets, Saints, Heaven and Hell.*
Naples, S. Maria Donnaregina. *After 1308.*

159. ASSISTANT OF CAVALLINI: *Detail from fresco of Last Judgement: Angels blowing trumpets.*
Naples, S. Maria Donnaregina. *After 1308.*

160. ASSISTANT OF CAVALLINI: *Detail from fresco of Last Judgement: The Elect entering Heaven.*
Naples, S. Maria Donnaregina. *After 1308.*

161. WORKSHOP OF CAVALLINI: *Fresco: S. Agnes taken to the brothel*. Detail.
Naples, S. Maria Donnaregina. *After 1308*.

162. WORKSHOP OF CAVALLINI: *Fresco: Christ nailed to the Cross*. Naples, S. Maria Donnaregina. *After 1308*.

163. IMMEDIATE FOLLOWER OF CAVALLINI: *S. John Evangelist taking leave of the Virgin.*
London, Mrs. Maurice Ephrussi.

164. IMMEDIATE FOLLOWER OF CAVALLINI: *The Death of the Virgin.* Detail.
London, Mrs. Maurice Ephrussi.

165–6. IMMEDIATE FOLLOWER OF CAVALLINI: *Frescoes: Creation of Eve.* Perugia, Palazza dei Priori.—
Expulsion from Paradise. Stimigliano, S. Maria in Vescovio.

167. IMMEDIATE FOLLOWER OF CAVALLINI: *Frescoes: Last Judgement and Scenes from the Old and New Testaments.*
Stimigliano, S. Maria in Vescovio.

168. IMMEDIATE FOLLOWER OF CAVALLINI: *Fresco: S. Michael defeats Satan.*
Detail. Florence, S. Croce.

169. IMMEDIATE FOLLOWER OF CAVALLINI: *Fresco: Miracle of the Bull on Mount Gargano.* Detail.
Florence, S. Croce.

170–1. RIMINESE FOLLOWER OF CAVALLINI AND GIOTTO: *Two details from detached fresco of Last Judgement.*
Rimini, Palazzo dell'Arengo.

2. RIMINESE FOLLOWER OF CAVALLINI AND GIOTTO: *Fresco: S. John Evangelist stops the earthquake at Ephesus.*
Rimini, S. Agostino.

173. GIULIANO DA RIMINI: *Dossal*. Boston, Isabella Stewart Gardner Museum. *Signed and dated 1307.*

174. RIMINESE ARTIST, XIV CENTURY: *Fresco: S. Guido pours out water for himself and transforms water into wine for his guest Gebeardo, archbishop of Ravenna.* Pomposa, S. Maria. *1316–20.*

175. RIMINESE ARTIST, XIV CENTURY: *Fresco: Three Saints*. Bagnacavallo, S. Pietro in Silvis.

176. GIOVANNI DA RIMINI: *Crucifix*. Mercatello, S. Francesco. *Signed and dated 13 (09? or 14?).*

177. Giovanni da Rimini: *Leaf of diptych: Presentation, Coronation of the Virgin, Scene from the life of S. Catherine, S. Francis receiving stigmata, S. John Baptist in the wilderness.* Alnwick Castle, Duke of Northumberland.

178. RIMINESE ARTIST, XIV CENTURY: *Frescoed vault: Four Evangelists and four Fathers of the Church.*
Ravenna, S. Maria in Porto Fuori. Destroyed 1944.

179. RIMINESE ARTIST, XIV CENTURY: *Frescoed triumphal arch: Christ as Judge; on His right, two Saints beheaded by the Antichrist, and the Elect; on His left, S. Michael beheads the Antichrist, and the Damned.* Ravenna, S. Maria in Porto Fuori. Destroyed in 1944.

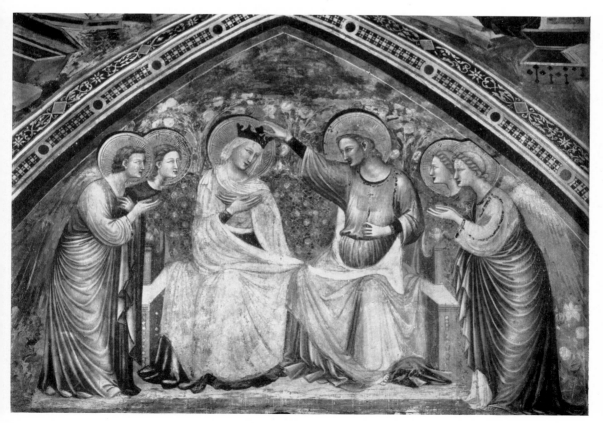

180. RIMINESE ARTIST, XIV CENTURY: *Fresco: Coronation of the Virgin.* Ravenna, S. Maria in Porto Fuori, Destroyed in 1944.

181–2. RIMINESE ARTIST, XIV CENTURY: *Fresco: Angel and Virgin of the Annunciation*. Ravenna, S. Chiara.

183. RIMINESE ARTIST, XIV CENTURY: *Fresco: Seated man in meditation (so-called Dante)*. Ravenna, S. Francesco.

184. RIMINESE ARTIST, XIV CENTURY: *Fresco: Nativity* Detail. Ravenna, S. Chiara.

185. Pietro da Rimini: *Crucifix*. Urbania, Chiesa dei Morti. *Signed*.

186. RIMINESE ARTIST, XIV CENTURY: *Deposition*. Paris, Louvre.

187. RIMINESE ARTIST, XIV CENTURY: *Fresco: Crucifixion with five Saints*. Tolentino, Basilica di S. Nicola.

188. Riminese artist, XIV century: *Fresco: S. Nicholas of Bari announces the birth of S. Nicholas of Tolentino*. Tolentino, Basilica di S. Nicola.

189. Riminese artist, XIV century: *Fresco: S. Nicholas of Tolentino saves a ship at sea*. Tolentino, Basilica di S. Nicola.

190. Riminese artist, XIV century: *Frescoes: Life of the Virgin and Christ in lunette and upper registers, Life and miracles of S. Nicholas of Tolentino*

192. RIMINESE ARTIST, XIV CENTURY: *Fresco: Christ disputing with the Doctors.* Detail. Tolentino, Basilica di S. Nicola.

191. RIMINESE ARTIST, XIV CENTURY: *Fresco: Christ in Limbo.* Detail. Tolentino, Basilica di S. Nicola.

193. RIMINESE ARTIST, XIV CENTURY: *Fresco: Marriage at Cana with two donors.* Detail.
Tolentino, Basilica di S. Nicola.

194. GIOVANNI BARONZIO DA RIMINI: *Coronation of the Virgin*. Detail.
New Haven (Conn.), Yale University Art Gallery.

195. RIMINESE ARTIST, XIV CENTURY: *Dossal: Deposition, Mourning over the Dead Christ, Resurrection, Descent into Limbo, Ascension, Descent of the Holy Ghost*. Rome, Galleria Nazionale, Palazzo Barberini.

196. GIOVANNI BARONZIO DA RIMINI: Polyptych: Madonna enthroned and Child, SS. Francis and Louis of Toulouse, and two Angels; Nativity, Circumcision, Last Supper, Betrayal of Christ; in pinnacles Crucifixion Angel and Virgin of Annunciation, four Saints. Urbino, Galleria Nazionale delle Marche. Signed and dated 1345.

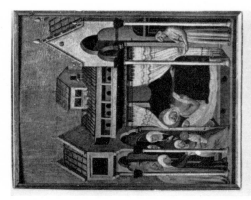

197. RIMINESE ARTIST, XIV CENTURY: *Reconstruction of dossal: Madonna and Child enthroned with four Angels and SS. Francis and Clare. Venice, Cini Collection.—Birth of the Virgin. Lausanne, Musée.—Annunciation, Circumcision, Dormition. Barcelona, Museo de Arte.*

198. RIMINESE ARTIST, XIV CENTURY: *Crucifix*. Verucchio, Collegiata.

199. RIMINESE ARTIST, XIV CENTURY (MASTER OF VERUCCHIO):
Pinnacle: Crucifixion with S. Francis. Strasbourg, Musée.

200–1. RIMINESE ARTIST, XIV CENTURY (MASTER OF VERUCCHIO): *Crucifixion and Noli me tangere.*
Dublin, National Gallery of Ireland.—*Madonna and Child enthroned with Saint and donor;*
below, SS. Louis of Toulouse, Marino and Clare. Formerly Lyons, Aynard Collection.

202. RIMINESE ARTIST, XIV CENTURY (MASTER OF THE URBINO CORONATION, PL. 204): *Frescoed lunette: Madonna and Child with SS. James, Dominic, Peter Martyr and Leonard, and donor.* Fano, S. Domenico.

203. FRANCESCO DA RIMINI: *Fragment of fresco: Risen Christ.* Bologna, S. Francesco. *Formerly signed.*

204. RIMINESE ARTIST, XIV CENTURY: *Detail of fragmentary polyptych: Coronation of the Virgin with SS. Catherine of Alexandria and Agnes.* Urbino, Galleria Nazionale delle Marche.

205. RIMINESE ARTIST, XIV CENTURY: *Panel of dossal: Herod's Feast.* New York, Robert Lehman.

207. Nuzi: *Madonna and Child enthroned with six Angels*. Agen, Musée.

206. Nuzi: *Madonna and Child enthroned*. Homeless.

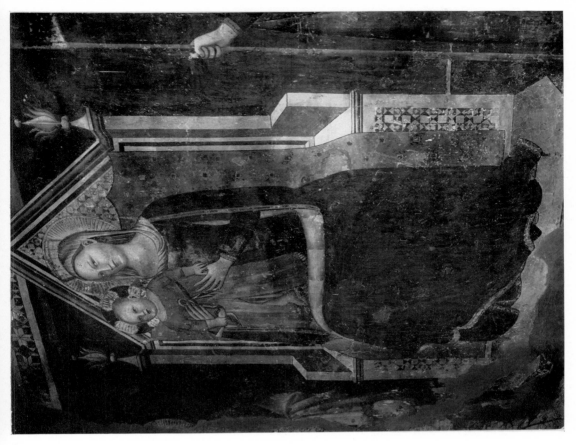

209. Nuzi: *Fresco: Madonna and Child enthroned.* Fabriano, S. Venanzio.

208. Nuzi: *Detail of polyptych: SS. Francis and Lucy.* Apiro, Palazzo Municipale. *Signed and dated 1366.*

210. NUZI: *Fall of Simon Magus.* Formerly London, George Farrow.

211. NUZI: *Scene of martyrdom.* Fragment. Homeless.

212–13. NUZI: *Two panels of dismembered dossal: Miracles of S. John Evangelist.*
New York, Mrs. W. Murray Crane. *Late work.*

214. NUZI(?): *Triptych: Coronation of the Virgin with Angels and Saints; in pinnacles, Angel and Virgin of the Annunciation.* Southampton, Art Gallery.

215. NUZI: *Madonna and Child enthroned.*
Urbino, Galleria Nazionale delle Marche.
Signed and dated 1372.

216. GHISSI: *Madonna of Humility suckling the Child.* Rome, Vatican Pinacoteca.

217. GHISSI: *Madonna of Humility and Angel.* Montegiorgio,
S. Salvatore. *Signed and dated 1374.*

218. ALTICHIERO: *Fresco: Crucifixion*. Detail. Padua, Basilica del Santo.

219. ALTICHIERO: *Fresco: Coronation of the Virgin with two kneeling warriors.*
Padua, Eremitani, Cappella Dotto. *Not before 1370.* (Destroyed 1944.)

220. ALTICHIERO: *Fresco: Wild bulls carry the body of S. James into the palace of Queen Lupa at Compostella.* Detail. Padua, Basilica del Santo. *1379.*

221. ALTICHIERO: *Frescoed lunette: The disciples of S. James are freed from prison by an Angel and their pursuers precipitated into a ravine.* Detail. Padua, Basilica del Santo. *1379*

222. ALTICHIERO: *Fresco: S. Lucy before Pascasius*. Padua, Oratorio di S. Giorgio. *1377–84*.

223. ALTICHIERO: *Fresco: The Beheading of S. George.* Padua, Oratorio di S. Giorgio. *1377–84.*

224. ALTICHIERO: *Fresco: Adoration of the Shepherds.* Detail. Padua, Oratorio di S. Giorgio. *1377–84.*

225. ALTICHIERO: *Fresco: Saints recommending members of the Cavalli family to the Madonna and Child.* Detail.
Verona, S. Anastasia. *After 1390.*

226. ALTICHIERO: *Fresco: Portrait of Petrarch.* (Background added later.) Padua, Liviano.

227. GIUSTO DE'MENABUOI: *Detail of outside wings of portable triptych: Meeting of Joachim and Anne at the Golden Gate, Birth, Presentation and Marriage of the Virgin*. London, National Gallery. *Signed and dated 1367*.

228. Giusto de'Menabuoi: *Detail of polyptych: Madonna and Child enthroned.* Padua, Baptistery. *1376.*

229. GIUSTO DE'MENABUOI: *Detail of fresco: Scenes from the Apocalypse*. Padua, Apse of Baptistery.
Cf. plate 235. *1376*.

230. GIUSTO DE'MENABUOI: *Polyptych and frescoes*. Padua, Baptistery. *1376*.

231–2. GIUSTO DE'MENABUOI: *Details of frescoes: King Herod watching the Massacre of the Innocents; Joseph and Mary watching Christ disputing with the Doctors.* Padua, Baptistery. *1376.*

233. GIUSTO DE'MENABUOI: *Frescoed lunette: Coronation of the Virgin and two kneeling donors recommended by Saints; Blessing Redeemer; Angel and Virgin of the Annunciation.* Padua, Basilica del Santo. *1380.*

234. GIUSTO DE'MENABUOI: *Frescoed wall: Scenes from the life of the Virgin and the life of Christ.* Padua, Baptistery. *1376.*

235. GIUSTO DE'MENABUOI: *Fresco: Madonna suckling the Child.*
Detail. Padua, Cappella degli Scrovegni.

236. GIUSTO DE'MENABUOI: *Fresco: Massacre of the Innocents.* Detail. Padua, Baptistery. *1376*.

237. GUARIENTO: *Crucifix with female donor*. Bassano del Grappa, Museo Civico.
Signed. Early work.

238. GUARIENTO: *Details from polyptych: Noli me tangere, Descent of the Holy Ghost.* Vienna, Czernin Collection.

98.

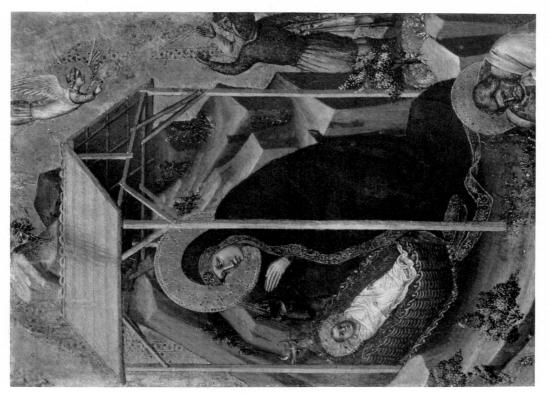

240. GUARIENTO: *Nativity*. Fragment. Homeless.

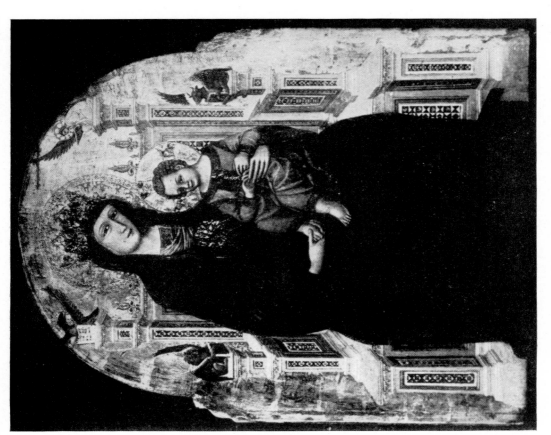

239. GUARIENTO: *Madonna and Child enthroned*. Homeless.

241. GUARIENTO: *Madonna and Child enthroned*. London, Courtauld Institute Galleries.

242. GUARIENTO: *Fragment from the ceiling of the Carraresi Chapel:*
Ten Angels holding lilies and globes. Padua, Museo Civico.

243–4. GUARIENTO: *Fragments from the ceiling of the Carraresi Chapel:*
Angel weighing a soul. Padua, Museo Civico.—*Angel with shield and spear.* Homeless.

245. GUARIENTO: *Monochrome allegory: Moon or Infancy*. Padua, Eremitani.

246–7. GUARIENTO: *Frescoes: SS. Mary Magdalen and Ursula, and Scenes from the Old Testament*.
Padua, Eremitani.

248. GUARIENTO: *Fresco: Christ and the Evangelists*. Detail. Padua, Eremitani.

249. GUARIENTO: *Fresco: God speaking to Adam and Eve*. Padua, Accademia.

250. GUARIENTO: *Fresco: Vision of young S. Augustine*. Padua, Eremitani.

251. GUARIENTO: *Monochrome fresco: Ecce homo*. Padua, Eremitani.

252. ANDREA DA BOLOGNA: *Madonna of Humility*
suckling the Child. Pausola, S. Agostino.
Signed and dated 1372.

253. ANDREA DA BOLOGNA: *Frescoes: S. Catherine consults the hermit; Mystic Marriage of S. Catherine.*
Detail. Offida, S. Maria della Rocca.

254. ANDREA DA BOLOGNA: Polyptych: Madonna and Child enthroned, with Crucifixion above; Zacharias in the Temple, Meeting at the Golden Gate, Birth of the Baptist, Naming of the Baptist, Baptism of Christ, SS. Francis and Anthony Abbot recommending nuns to the Virgin, Two visions of S. John Evangelist and three Stories of a Bishop Saint. Fermo, Museum. Signed and dated 1368.

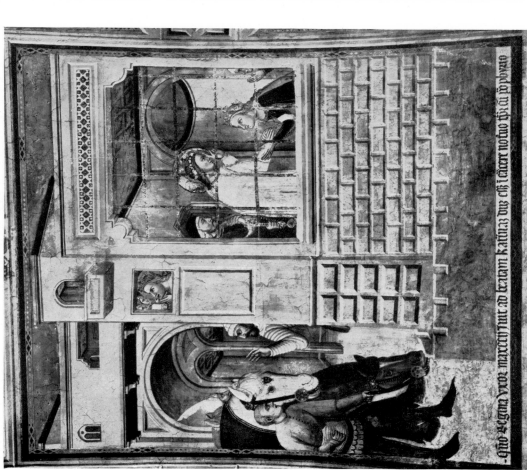

255–6. ANDREA DA BOLOGNA: *Frescoes*: *S. Catherine in prison; Martyrdom and Assumption of S. Catherine. Assisi, S. Francesco, Lower Church.*

257. Tomaso da Modena: *Eight panels of reliquary diptych: Symbols of the Evangelists,*
S. Francis and S. Michael, four half-length Saints. Baltimore, Walters Art Gallery.

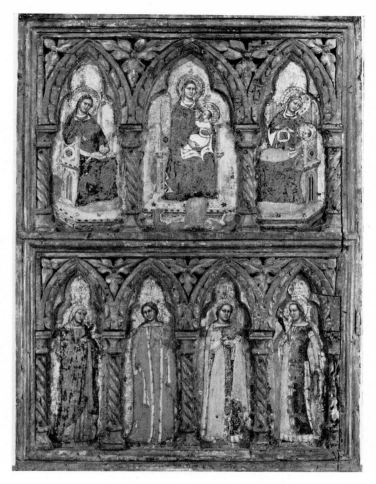

258. TOMASO DA MODENA: *Detail from portable altarpiece:*
Madonna reading, Madonna and Child enthroned, Madonna dressing the Child;
below, SS. Anastasia, Lucy, Agnes and Catherine.
Bologna, Pinacoteca. *Before 1349.*

259. TOMASO DA MODENA: *Detail from portable triptych: Christ in Limbo, the young S. John Baptist in*
the wilderness, S. Catherine. Modena, Pinacoteca Estense. *Signed and dated 13(?)5.*

260. TOMASO DA MODENA: *Fresco: Cardinal reading with the aid of a magnifying glass.*
Treviso, Seminario. *Signed and dated 1352.*

261. TOMASO DA MODENA: *Detail from detached frescoes of the Legend of S. Ursula: The English king gives instructions to the departing ambassadors.* Treviso, Museo Civico. *Late work.*

262. Tomaso da Modena: *Votive fresco: S. Jerome in his study*. Treviso, S. Niccolò.

263. VITALE DA BOLOGNA: *Panel of polyptych: S. Peter blessing a pilgrim.*
Bologna, Collezioni Comunali. *1345.*

264. VITALE DA BOLOGNA: *Madonna and Child worshipped by Pope and Cardinal.*
Viterbo, Museo Civico.

265. VITALE DA BOLOGNA: *Fresco from Mezzaratta: Nativity*. Detail. Bologna, Pinacoteca.

266–8. VITALE DA BOLOGNA: *Three scenes from the life of S. Anthony Abbot.* (Possibly side-panels of a dispersed, signed altarpiece in S. Antonio.)
Bologna, Pinacoteca

270. VITALE DA BOLOGNA: *S. George killing the dragon. Bologna, Pinacoteca. Signed.*

269. VITALE DA BOLOGNA: *Fresco: S. Eustace is baptized with his family. Pomposa, Abbazia. Dated 1351.*

271. BARNABA DA MODENA: *Madonna and Child*. Formerly Berlin, Staatliche Museen.
Signed and dated 1369.

272. BARNABA DA MODENA: *Nativity*.
Bologna, Collezioni Comunali.

273. BARNABA DA MODENA: *The Trinity with the symbols of the Evangelists*. London, National Gallery.

274. BARNABA DA MODENA: *Madonna and Child*.
Homeless.

275. BARNABA DA MODENA: *Madonna and Child*.
London, Courtauld Institute Galleries. *Signed*.

276. BARNABA DA MODENA: *Baptism of Christ*. Algiers, Musée.

277. BARNABA DA MODENA: *Portable altarpiece: Madonna and Child with SS. John Baptist and Catherine; Crucifixion; Angel and Virgin of the Annunciation*. Modena, Pinacoteca Estense. *Signed*.

278. BARNABA DA MODENA: *Predella panel: Annunciation*. Altenburg, Lindenau Museum.

279. BARNABA DA MODENA: *Centre panel of polyptych: Madonna and Child enthroned with eight* **Angels.**
Pisa, Museo Nazionale di S. Matteo. *Signed. About 1380.*

280. BARNABA DA MODENA AND NICCOLÒ DA VOLTRI: *Triptych: Madonna and Child, S. Catherine and S. Nicholas with donors; above, Crucifixion and Saints. Genoa, Palazzo Bianco. Signed by Barnaba.*

281. NICCOLÒ DA VOLTRI: *Madonna suckling the Child, with two Angels and two worshippers.* Baltimore, Walters Art Gallery.

282. NICCOLÒ DA VOLTRI: *Madonna and Child.* Genoa, S. Donato. *Signed.*

283. Niccolò da Voltri: *Polyptych from the Chiesa delle Vigne, Genoa: Annunciation; S. John Baptist,*
Angel Raphael with Tobias; S. Dominic and S. Paul; Trinity worshipped by the Virgin and S. John Baptist;
Bishop Saint and Apostle. Rome, Vatican Pinacoteca. *Signed and dated 1401.*

284. LIPPO DALMASIO: *Detail from centre panel of portable altarpiece: Coronation of the Virgin.* Bologna, Pinacoteca. *Signed and dated 1394.*

285. LIPPO DALMASIO: *Madonna and Child enthroned.* Norton Hall, Capt. W. M. H. Pollen. *Signed and dated 1409.*

286. LIPPO DALMASIO: *Fresco: Madonna suckling the Child and four Angels.* Pistoia, Museo. *Dated 1407.*

287. LIPPO DALMASIO: *Madonna suckling the Child*. Bologna, Pinacoteca. *Signed.*

287a. TRAINI: *A Bishop Saint*. Detail. Florence, Gallerie Fiorentine.

288. TRAINI: *Pinnacle: Blessing Redeemer.* Chapel Hill, N.C., Ackland Art Center.

289. TRAINI: *Panel of polyptych: S. Gregory.* Homeless.

290. TRAINI: *Right panel of polyptych: S. Paul.* Nancy, Musée.

291. Traini: *Madonna and Child with S. Anne*. Princeton, N.J., University Art Museum.

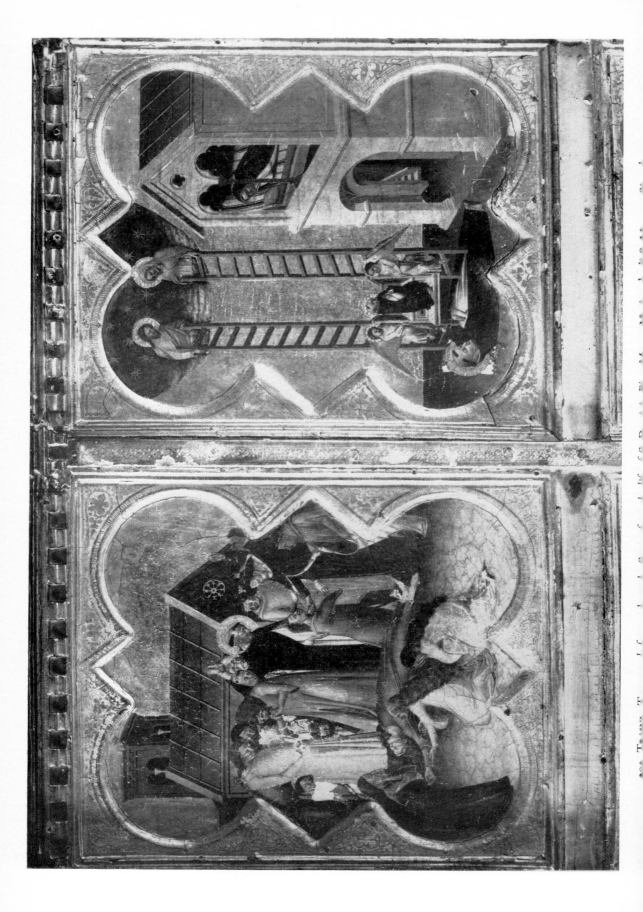

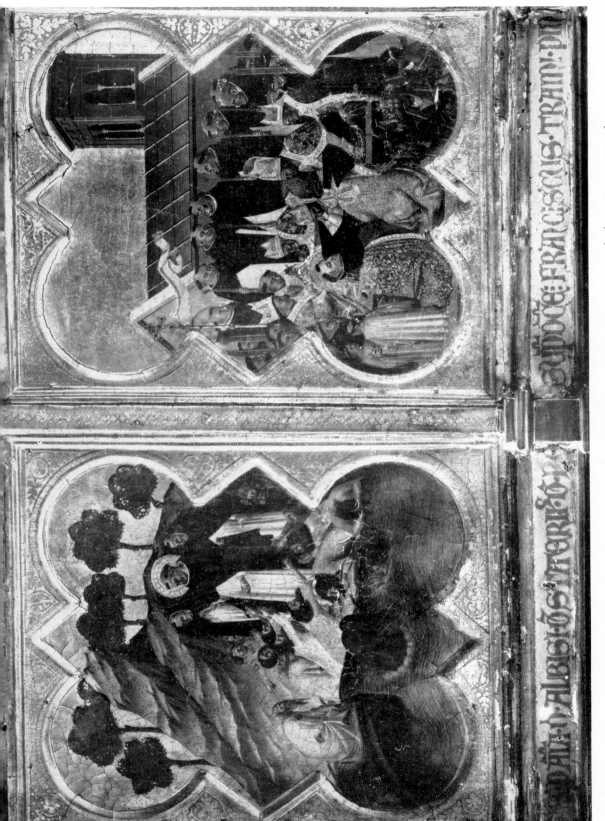

293. TRAINI: *Two panels from polyptych: Scenes from the life of S. Dominic. Pisa, Museo Nazionale di S. Matteo. Signed. 1345.*

296. TRAINI: *Detail from detached fresco of Thebaid: Temptation of a hermit.* Pisa, Camposanto, Museo.

295. TRAINI: *Detail from detached fresco of the Last Judgement: Angel guiding a soul to Heaven.* Pisa, Camposanto, Museo.

297. TRAINI: *Detail from detached fresco of the Triumph of Death: Demons torturing the damned. Pisa, Camposanto, Museo.*

298. TRAINI: *Detail from detached fresco of the Triumph of Death: Three coffins*. Pisa, Camposanto, Museo.

299. Between Traini and Lippo Memmi: *Detail from the Triumph of S. Thomas Aquinas: Christ in mandorla.*
Pisa, S. Caterina.

300. LIPPO MEMMI (and his father MEMMO?): *Fresco: Maestà.* Detail. San Gimignano, Palazzo del Popolo.
Signed and dated 1317.

301-2. LIPPO MEMMI: *Side-panels to Simone Martini's Annunciation: S. Ansanus, S. Margaret.*
Florence, Uffizi. *1333.*

303. LIPPO MEMMI: *Madonna and Child with donor*. Washington, National Gallery of Art, Mellon Collection.

304. LIPPO MEMMI: *Left panel of diptych: Madonna and Child; above, the Angel of the Annunciation*. Detail. Berlin, Staatliche Museen. *Signed*.

305. LIPPO MEMMI: *Madonna and Child on draped throne*. Altenburg, Lindenau Museum. *Signed.*

306. LIPPO MEMMI: '*Madonna del Popolo*'. Siena, S. Maria dei Servi.

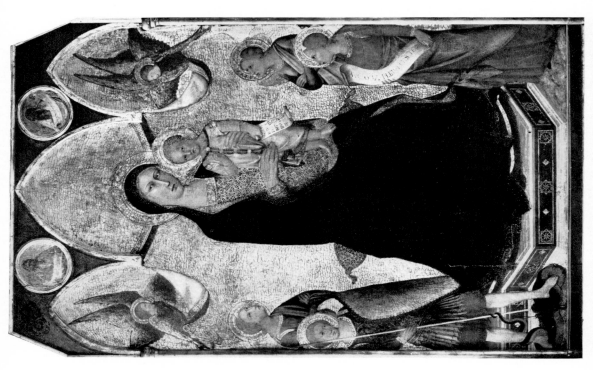

307–309. CLOSE IMITATOR OF SIMONE MARTINI (MASTER OF THE PALAZZO VENEZIA MADONNA): Triptych: Madonna and Child enthroned

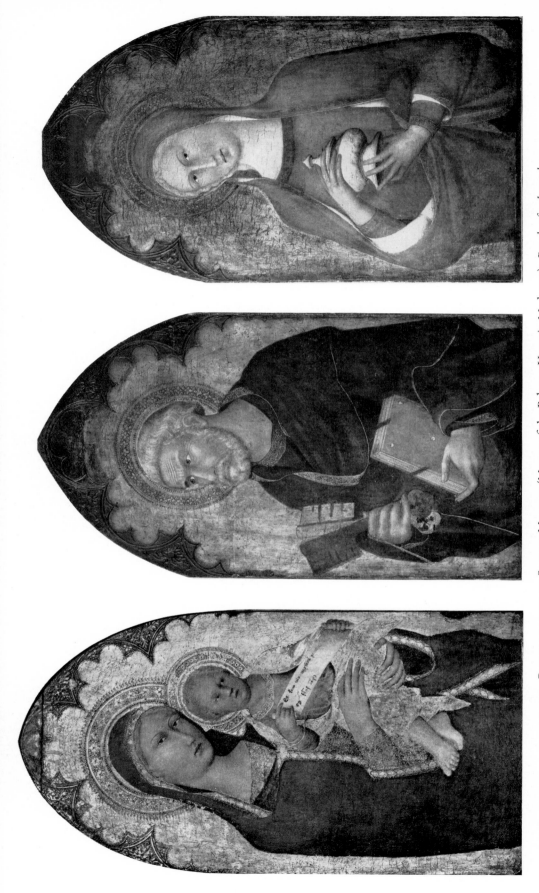

310–12. CLOSE IMITATOR OF SIMONE MARTINI (Master of the Palazzo Venezia Madonna): *Panels of polyptych: Madonna and Child.* Rome, Museo di Palazzo Venezia.—*SS. Peter and Mary Magdalen.* London, National Gallery.

315. CLOSE IMITATOR OF SIMONE MARTINI:
Right panel of polyptych: S. John Evangelist.
New Haven, Yale University Gallery.

314. CLOSE IMITATOR OF SIMONE MARTINI:
'Straus' *Madonna.* Houston, Texas, Museum of Art.

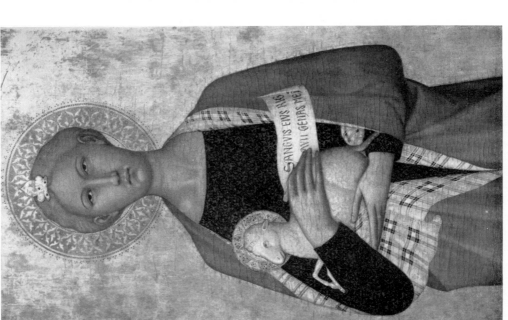

313. CLOSE IMITATOR OF SIMONE MARTINI:
Side-panel of triptych: S. Agnes. Worcester, Mass.,
Museum of Art.

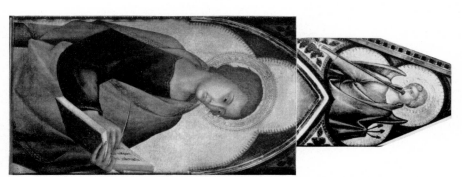

316-18. LIPPO MEMMI: Panels of polyptych: Madonna and Child; in pinnacle, Christ as Judge. Siena, Pinacoteca.—SS. John Evangelist and Peter; in pinnacles, Angels blowing trumpets and holding Instruments of the Passion. Homeless.

319. CECCARELLI: *Polyptych: Madonna and Child, SS. Anthony Abbot, Michael, John Evangelist and Stephen; in pinnacles, Redeemer and Angels. Siena, Pinacoteca.*

320. CECCARELLI: *Madonna and Child. Richmond, Cook Collection. Signed and dated 1347.*

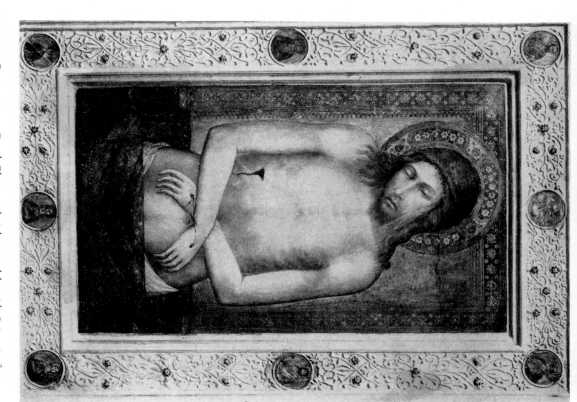

321. CECCARELLI: *Dead Christ and eight roundels with Saints in frame. Vaduz, Liechtenstein Collection.*

322. CECCARELLI: *Portable altarpiece: Madonna and Child holding scroll; SS. Eligius(?) and Bartholomew; SS. Nicholas and Anthony Abbot; Angel and Virgin of the Annunciation.* Tyninghame, Earl of Haddington.

323. GIOVANNI DI NICOLA DA PISA: *Polyptych: Madonna and Child, SS. Bona, John Baptist, Mary Magdalen and Bartholomew; in pinnacles, blessing Redeemer and four busts of Saints.* Pisa, Museo Nazionale di S. Matteo. *Signed and dated 13(50?).*

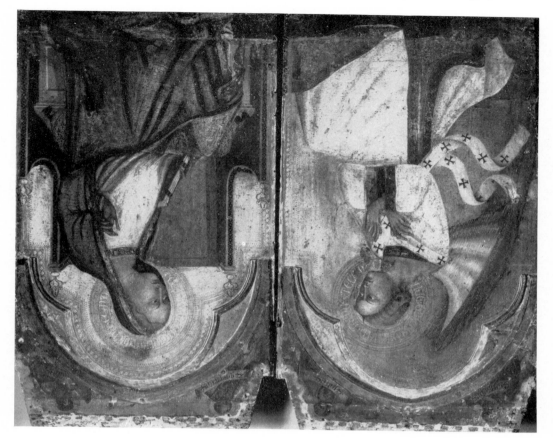

326. GIOVANNI DI NICOLA DA PISA: *Pinnacles: Angel and Virgin of the Annunciation.*
Pisa, Seminario Vescovile.

325. GIOVANNI DI NICOLA DA PISA: *Madonna of Humility.*
Venice, Ca' d'Oro.

324. GIOVANNI DI NICOLA DA PISA: *Madonna.*
Homeless.

327. BARNA DA SIENA (?): *Exvoto of Arrigo di Neri Arrighetti: Mystic Marriage of S. Catherine, and the Virgin and S. Anne playing with the Infant Jesus; below, S. Margaret defeating the dragon, Reconciliation of two knights, S. Michael killing the Devil*. Boston, Museum of Fine Arts.

328-9. BARNA DA SIENA: *Christ carrying the Cross; Christ on the Cross.*
Formerly Frankfurt, Harry Fuld.

330. BARNA DA SIENA: *Christ carrying the Cross and a Dominican donor.*
New York, Frick Collection.

331. BARNA DA SIENA: *Centre panel of a polyptych: Madonna and Child with donor*. Detail.
Asciano, Museo d'Arte Sacra.

332. BARNA DA SIENA: *Detail of fresco: Christ on the way to Calvary*. San Gimignano, Collegiata.

333. BARNA DA SIENA: *Frescoed wall: Scenes from the life of Christ*. San Gimignano, Collegiata.

334. BARNA DA SIENA: *Detail of fresco: Agony in the Garden.*
San Gimignano, Collegiata.

335. BARNA DA SIENA: *Detail of fresco: Agony in the Garden.* San Gimignano, Collegiata.

336–7. BARNA DA SIENA(?): *Diptych: Annunciation with kneeling Dominican; below, six Saints.*
Berlin-Dahlem, Staatliche Museen.—*Crucifixion and Mourning over Christ.* Oxford, Ashmolean Museum.

338–9. LIPPO VANNI: *Two panels of polyptych: Madonna and Child.* New York, Robert Lehman.—
S. Luke. Geneva, Lederer Collection.

340. LIPPO VANNI: *Miniature from antiphonary: Ecstasy of S. Mary Magdalen.*
Siena, Seminario.

341. LIPPO VANNI: *Predella panel: Dormition*. Detail. Altenburg, Lindenau Museum.

342. LIPPO VANNI: *Centre panel of triptych: Madonna and Child with donors.* Coral Gables, Fla.,
Lowe Art Gallery, Kress Collection.

343. LIPPO VANNI: *Miniature from a gradual: Birth of the Virgin.*
Siena, Opera del Duomo. *1345.*

344. LIPPO VANNI: *Illuminated initial: Christ opens the eyes of the Apostles.* Saltwood Castle, Sir Kenneth Clark.

345. LIPPO VANNI: *Miniature: S. Francis in initial I.* Formerly Amsterdam, N. Beets Collection.

346. LIPPO VANNI: *Frescoes in apse*. San Leonardo al Lago near Siena.

347. LIPPO VANNI: *Madonna and Child*. Fragment.
Perugia, Galleria Nazionale dell'Umbria.
About 1355.

348. LIPPO VANNI: *Madonna and Child
with goldfinch and two Angels*. Fragment.
Le Mans, Musée.

349. LIPPO VANNI: *Predella panel: S. Monica and S. Augustine*. Homeless.

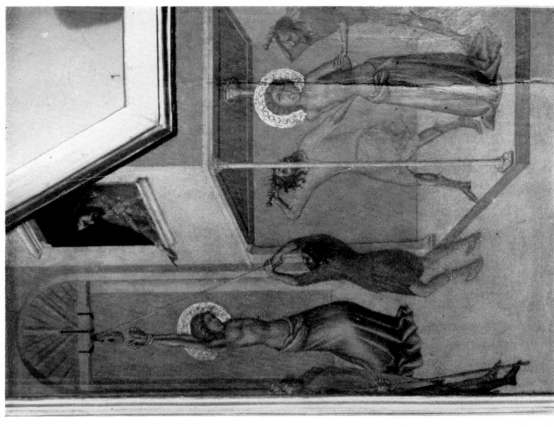

350–1. LIPPO VANNI: *Two details from a reliquary triptych: Madonna and Child enthroned; Scene from the life of S. Aurea.*

352. LIPPO VANNI: *Monochrome fresco: Victory of the Sienese over Nicola da Montefeltro in 1363 in the Val di Chiana. Detail. Signed and dated 1373.—* *Below: S. Bernardino by Sano di Pietro. 1451.—S. Catherine of Siena by Vecchietta. Signed and dated 1461. Siena, Palazzo Pubblico.*

354. Niccolò di Buonaccorso: *Madonna of Humility.*
Homeless.

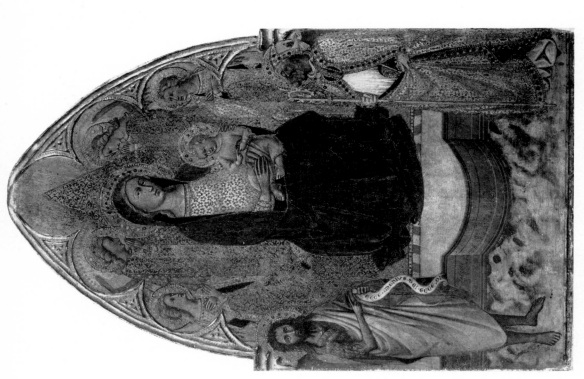

353. Niccolò di Buonaccorso: *Madonna and Child enthroned
with SS. John Baptist, Augustine and four Angels.*

356. Niccolò di Buonaccorso: *Coronation of the Virgin.*
New York, Robert Lehman.

355. Niccolò di Buonaccorso: *Marriage of the Virgin.*
London, National Gallery. *Signed.*

357. NICCOLÒ DI SER SOZZO TEGLIACCI:
Panel of dismembered polyptych: Virgin of the Assumption. Fragment.
San Gimignano, Museo d'Arte Sacra.

358. NICCOLÒ DI SER SOZZO TEGLIACCI:
Madonna and Child holding pomegranate.
Florence, Uffizi.

359. NICCOLÒ DI SER SOZZO TEGLIACCI:
Madonna and Child with two Angels. Fragment.
Greenwich (Conn.), T. S. Hyland Collection.

60. Niccolò di Ser Sozzo Tegliacci: *Illuminated frontispiece: 'Caleffo dell'Assunta'*. Siena, Archivio di Stato.
Signed.

361. NICCOLÒ DI SER SOZZO TEGLIACCI: *Miniature: S. Gimignanus enthroned with four Angels and six worshipping monks.* San Gimignano, Museo d'Arte Sacra.

362. NICCOLÒ DI SER SOZZO TEGLIACCI: *Miniature: Resurrection.* San Gimignano, Museo d'Arte Sacra.

363. NICCOLÒ DI SER SOZZO TEGLIACCI: *Illuminated init Virgin of the Assumption.* Newark, N. J., Newark Museu

364. LUCA DI TOMMÈ: *Polyptych: Madonna and Child with S. Anne; SS. Catherine,*
John Baptist, Anthony Abbot and Apollonia (?); in pinnacles, S. Andrew and the four Evangelists.
Siena, Pinacoteca. Signed and dated 1367.

365. NICCOLÒ DI SER SOZZO TEGLIACCI AND LUCA DI TOMMÈ: *Polyptych: Madonna and Child enthroned*
with six Angels, SS. John Baptist, Thomas, Benedict and Stephen. Siena, Pinacoteca.
Signed by both artists and dated 1362.

366–7. NICCOLÒ DI SER SOZZO TEGLIACCI AND LUCA DI TOMMÈ: *Two predella panels:*
The King of India offers S. Thomas a banquet, and a dog brings in the hand that slapped the Saint;
S. Thomas in prison converts the King's brother, is liberated and baptizes the King.
Balcarres, Earl of Crawford and Balcarres. *1362.*

368. Luca di Tommè: *Assumption of the Virgin*. Detail. New Haven, Conn., Yale University Art Gallery.

369. LUCA DI TOMMÈ: *Crucifixion*. Pisa, Museo Nazionale di S. Matteo.
Signed and dated 1366.

370. LUCA DI TOMMÈ:
Panel of polyptych: S. Stephen.
Homeless.

371. LUCA DI TOMMÈ: *Centre panel
of polyptych: Madonna and Child.*
New York, Metropolitan Museum.

372. LUCA DI TOMMÈ:
Panel of polyptych: S. John Baptist.
Florence, Museo Bardini.

373. LUCA DI TOMMÈ: *Detail of polyptych: Madonna and Child, SS. Peter, Paul, Dominic and Peter Martyr.*
Rieti, Museo. *Signed and dated 1370.*

374. PUCCINELLI: *Triptych: S. Michael enthroned, S. Anthony Abbot, S. John Baptist; in pinnacles, blessing Redeemer, Angel and Virgin of the Annunciation. Siena, Pinacoteca. (1379?).*

375. PUCCINELLI: *Triptych: Marriage of S. Catherine; SS. Peter and John Baptist; SS. Gervasius and Protasius*. Lucca, Museo di Villa Guinigi. *Signed and dated 135(0?)*.

376–7. PUCCINELLI: *Details of polyptych: SS. Lucy and Nicholas; Madonna and Child*. Varano, Parish Church. *Signed and dated 1394*.

379. Giuliano di Simone da Lucca: *Madonna and Child enthroned with four adoring Angels, SS. Catherine, John Baptist, Francis, Virgin Martyr, and Eve below;*

378. Giuliano di Simone da Lucca: *Centre panel of polyptych: Madonna suckling the Child.*

381. GIULIANO DI SIMONE DA LUCCA: Madonna del Latte with four music-making Angels,
SS. Mary Magdalen, Nicholas, Dorothy and Peter, and Eve below. Paris, Louvre.

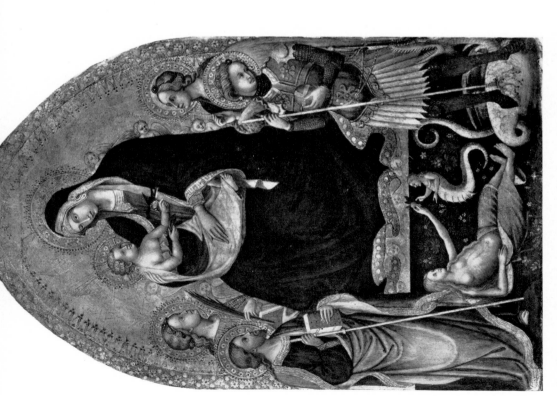

380. GIULIANO DI SIMONE DA LUCCA: Madonna and Child enthroned,
with S. James, S. Michael and two female Saints, and Eve below.
Formerly Leghorn, Larderel Collection.

383. FRANCESCO DI VANNUCCIO:
Panel of diptych: Annunciation with two donors.

382. FRANCESCO DI VANNUCCIO: *Detail of Reliquary.*
Formerly Berlin, R. von Kaufmann.

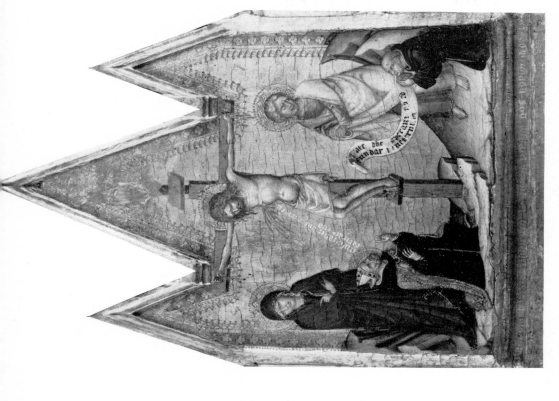

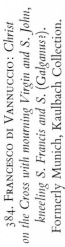

384. FRANCESCO DI VANNUCCIO: *Christ on the Cross with mourning Virgin and S. John, kneeling S. Francis and S. (Galganus?). Formerly Munich, Kaulbach Collection.*

385. FRANCESCO DI VANNUCCIO: *Christ on the Cross with mourning Virgin and S. John, Bishop Saint and monk. Berlin-Dahlem, Staatliche Museen. Signed and dated 137(0?).*

386. FRANCESCO DI VANNUCCIO: *Crucifix*. Greenville, S.C., Bob Jones University Museum.

387. ANDREA VANNI: *Madonna and Child, with Annunciation above.*
Homeless.

388. ANDREA VANNI: *Two pinnacles: Angel and Virgin of the Annunciation.* Cambridge, Mass.,
Fogg Art Museum.

389–90. ANDREA VANNI: *Two panels of polyptych: Resurrection*. Formerly Ingenheim,
Graf Ingenheim.—*Ascension*. Leningrad, Hermitage.

391. ANDREA VANNI: *Three panels of polyptych: Crucifixion, Agony in the Garden, Descent into Limbo.*
Washington, Corcoran Gallery of Art. *Signed. About 1383.*

392. ANDREA VANNI: *Portable altarpiece: Crucifixion; SS. Stephen and Anthony Abbot; SS. Catherine and John Baptist; in pinnacles, Blessing Redeemer, Angel and Virgin of the Annunciation.* Boston, Isabella Stewart Gardner Museum.

393. ANDREA VANNI: *Triptych: Crucifixion and four Prophets.* Siena, Pinacoteca. *1396.*

394. ANDREA VANNI: *Panel of polyptych: Evangelist*. New York, Dr. L. Malcove.

395. ANDREA VANNI: *Blessing Redeemer*. Formerly Pontedera, Toscanelli Collection

396–7. ANDREA VANNI: *Two panels of Casaluce polyptych: S. James*. Naples, Galleria Nazionale.—*S. Francis*. Altenburg, Lindenau Museum.

398. ANDREA VANNI: *Polyptych: Madonna and Child, fourteen Saints, Annunciation, the four Evangelists.*
(Predella by Giovanni di Paolo.) Siena, S. Stefano. *1400.*

399. GIACOMO DI MINO DEL PELLICCIAJO: *Portable altarpiece: Mystic Marriage of S. Catherine with four Angels, S. Ansanus, S. Mary Magdalen, S. Eulalia, and Annunciation*. Detail. Perugia, Galleria Nazionale dell'Umbria.

400–1. GIACOMO DI MINO DEL PELLICCIAJO: *Panels of polyptych: S. John Evangelist; S. John Baptist.*
Sarteano, S. Francesco.

402. GIACOMO DI MINO DEL PELLICCIAJO: *Detail of triptych: Madonna and Child with
SS. Mary Magdalen, Lucy, Agnes, Catherine, and six Angels; S. Anthony Abbot, S. Michael.*
Siena, Pinacoteca. *Signed and dated 1362.*

403. GIACOMO DI MINO DEL PELLICCIAJO:
Centre panel of triptych: Madonna and Child. Sarteano,
SS. Martino e Vittoria. *Signed and dated 13(42?).*

404. BARTOLO DI FREDI: *Madonna della Rosa.*
Cusona, S. Biagio. *Signed.*

405. BARTOLO DI FREDI: *Fresco: Joseph lowered into the well*. Detail. San Gimignano, Collegiata. *Signed and dated 1367.*

406. Bartolo di Fredi: *Frescoed wall: S. Francis receiving stigmata, S. Christopher crossing the stream with Jesus on his shoulder; Madonna and Child enthroned with Angels; S. George slaying the dragon; Adoration of the Magi.* Lucignano, S. Francesco.

407. Bartolo di Fredi: *Madonna of Mercy*. Pienza, Museo della Cattedrale.
Signed and dated 1364.

408. Bartolo di Fredi: *Fresco: Birth of the Virgin*. San Gimignano, S. Agostino. *1363.*

409. Bartolo di Fredi: *Adoration of the Magi*. Siena, Pinacoteca.

410. Bartolo di Fredi: *Triptych: Nativity, Bishop Saint, S. Anthony Abbot.*
Torrita, SS. Flora e Lucilla.

411–12. Bartolo di Fredi: *Fragments of polyptych: Levitation of Filippo Ciardelli; Baptism of Christ.*
Montalcino, Museo Civico. *Signed and dated 1382.*

413. Bartolo di Fredi: *Fragments of polyptych: The dying Virgin taking leave of the Apostles, Marriage of the Virgin, Death of the Virgin, the Virgin's return to her parents.* Siena, Pinacoteca. *1388.*

414. MASTER OF PANZANO TRIPTYCH: *Triptych: Mystic Marriage of S. Catherine, S. Paul, S. Peter; in pinnacles, blessing Redeemer, S. Anthony Abbot, S. Blaise.* Panzano, Pieve.

415. PAOLO DI GIOVANNI FEI: *Polyptych: Madonna and Child enthroned; S. Andrew, S. John Baptist, S. Francis and Prophet Daniel; in pillars, SS. Agnes, Margaret, Catherine, Nicholas, Bartholomew and James.* Siena, Pinacoteca. *Signed.*

416. PAOLO DI GIOVANNI FEI: *Birth of the Virgin, flanked by SS. James and Catherine, SS. Bartholomew and Elizabeth of Hungary; in pinnacles, Redeemer, Angel and Virgin of the Annunciation, and two Seraphim.* Siena, Pinacoteca.

417. PAOLO DI GIOVANNI FEI: *Portable triptych: Madonna and Child with two Angels and SS. Peter, Bartholomew, John Evangelist and Andrew; Christ on the Cross above; in wings, SS. Michael and Augustine, SS. Mary Magdalen and Catherine, and two Evangelists in roundels above.* Rome, Conte L. Vitetti.

418. Paolo di Giovanni Fei: *Presentation of the Virgin*. Detail. Washington, National Gallery of Art, Kress Collection.

419. PAOLO DI GIOVANNI FEI:
Madonna and Child with seven Angels.
Siena, S. Maria della Scala.

420. PAOLO DI GIOVANNI FEI:
Right panel of polyptych: S. Lawrence.
Homeless.

421. ANDREA DI BARTOLO: *Madonna of Humility
and two adoring Angels.* Homeless. *Signed.*

422. ANDREA DI BARTOLO: *Madonna of Humility
and two Angels.* Montreal, Museum of Fine Arts.

423. ANDREA DI BARTOLO: *Madonna della Cintola with Messer Palamedes
and his son Matteo*. Richmond, Va., Museum of Art. *Signed*.

424. ANDREA DI BARTOLO: *Painted casket with the four Patron Saints of Siena: Savinus, Crescentius, Victor and Ansanus*. Siena, Palazzo Pubblico. *1373*.

425–6. ANDREA DI BARTOLO: *S. Michael stops S. Galganus' horse*. Pisa, Museo Civico.—*The parents of S. Galganus cannot induce him to return home*. Dublin, National Gallery of Ireland.

427. ANDREA DI BARTOLO: *Predella panel: Crucifixion*. Budapest, Museum of Fine Arts.

428. ANDREA DI BARTOLO: *Mourning Virgin and S. John Evangelist*. Homeless.

429. ANDREA DI BARTOLO: *Massacre of the Innocents*. Baltimore, Walters Art Gallery.

430. ANDREA DI BARTOLO: *SS. Apollonia and Agatha*.
Formerly London, W. S. M. Burns.

431–2. ANDREA DI BARTOLO: *Two panels from pilaster
of polyptych: S. Margaret, S. Cecilia*. Homeless.

433. MARTINO DI BARTOLOMEO DA SIENA: *Triptych: SS. Stephen, Mary Magdalen, and Anthony Abbot; in pinnacles, Virgin and two Angels.* Siena, Palazzo Pubblico. *Formerly signed and dated 1408.*

434–6. MARTINO DI BARTOLOMEO DA SIENA: *Panels of polyptych: S. John Baptist with Angel of the Annunciation above. Homeless.—Christ enthroned. Formerly Perugia, Van Marle Collection.— S. Mary Magdalen with Virgin of the Annunciation above. Homeless.*

437. MARTINO DI BARTOLOMEO DA SIENA: *Madonna and Child.* Milan, Tullio Fossati Bellani. *Signed and dated 1408.*

438. MARTINO DI BARTOLOMEO DA SIENA: *Madonna and Child.* Homeless.

439. MARTINO DI BARTOLOMEO DA SIENA: *Coronation of the Virgin*.
Los Angeles, County Museum of Art.

440. MARTINO DI BARTOLOMEO DA SIENA: *Predella panel: Scene from the life of a Saint*. Philadelphia,
Museum of Art.

441–2. MARTINO DI BARTOLOMEO DA SIENA: *The infant S. Stephen stolen by the devil; the Finding of the abducted infant Saint.* Frankfurt, Staedel Institute.

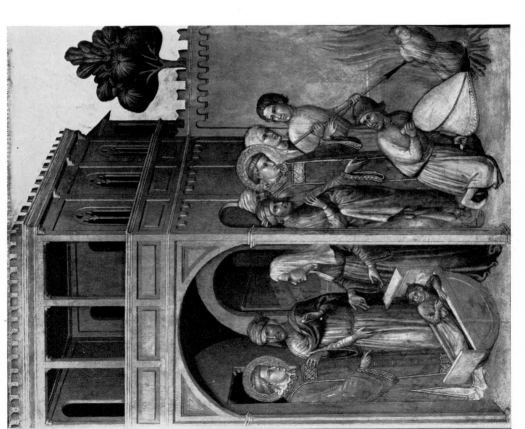

443–4. Martino di Bartolomeo da Siena: *S. Stephen exorcizing a changeling; S. Stephen destroying pagan idols*, Frankfurt, Staedel Institute.

445. Martino di Bartolomeo da Siena: *Polyptych: Madonna and Child, SS. Anthony Abbot, Bartholomew, John Baptist and Lucy; in pinnacles, Redeemer and four Saints. Pisa, Museo Nazionale di S. Matteo. Signed and dated 1403.*

446. Martino di Bartolomeo da Siena and Giovanni di Pietro da Napoli: *Polyptych: Madonna and Child enthroned; SS. Augustine and John Baptist, with Evangelist in roundel above; SS. John Evangelist and Clare, with Evangelist in roundel above.* Pisa, Museo Nazionale di S. Matteo. 1402.

447. Martino di Bartolomeo da Siena and Giovanni Pietro da Napoli: *Mystic Marriage of S. Catherine with kneeling donor*. Pisa, Museo Nazionale di S. Matteo. *Dated 1404.*

448. Giovanni di Pietro da Napoli: *Fresco: Christ on the Cross with mourning Virgin and S. John Evangelist, S. Francis and two donors*. Pisa, Museo Nazionale di S. Matteo. *Signed and dated 1405.*

449–51. Nanni di Jacopo: *Fragments of polyptych: SS. James and John Evangelist; Madonna and Child with six Ang SS. Michael and Anthony Abbot*. Rome, Palazzo Venezia. *Signed.*

452. NANNI DI JACOPO: *Polyptych: Madonna and Child with four music-making Angels; SS. James and Augustine; SS. Donnino and Anthony Abbot; in pinnacles, blessing Saviour, Angel and Virgin of the Annunciation; in predella, Dead Christ with mourning Virgin and S. John Evangelist, SS. Clare and Lucy; SS. John Baptist and Francis. Formerly Florence, Marchesa Panciatichi.*

453. Getto di Jacopo da Pisa: *S. Dominic surrounded by SS. Augustine, Bartholomew, Hilarion, John Baptist and John Evangelist; above, Annunciation and blessing Redeemer.* Pisa, Museo Nazionale di S. Matteo. *Signed and dated 1391.*

454. CECCO DI PIETRO: *Crucifixion*. Homeless.

455. CECCO DI PIETRO: *Madonna suckling the Child*. Fragment. Homeless.

456–7. CECCO DI PIETRO: *Pope with palm; S. Peter*. Homeless.

458. CECCO DI PIETRO: *Predella panel: Olibrius meets S. Margaret*. Pisa, Museo Nazionale di S. Matteo.

459. Cᴇᴄᴄᴏ ᴅɪ Pɪᴇᴛʀᴏ: *Centre panel of polyptych: Madonna and Child
enthroned, blessing two donors.* Portland, Ore., Art Museum,
Kress Collection. *Signed and dated 1386.*

461. GERA: *Madonna and Child flanked by SS. Lucy and Catherine.*
Volterra, Pinacoteca.

460. CECCO DI PIETRO: *Centre panel of polyptych: Madonna and Child
enthroned, with goldfinch. Copenhagen, Royal Museum. Signed.*

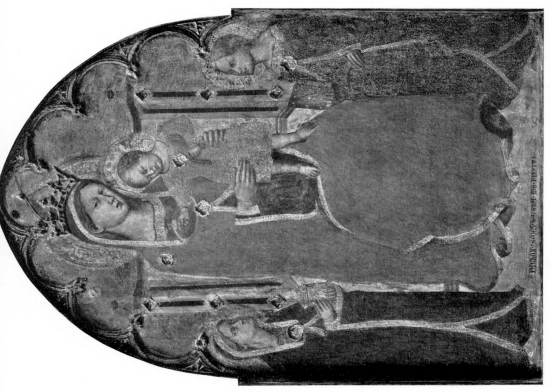

463. GERA: *Madonna and Child flanked by SS. Mary Magdalen and Margaret.*
Pisa, Museo Nazionale di S. Matteo. *Signed.*

462. GERA: *Madonna and Child flanked by SS. Francis and Anthony Abbot.*
Pisa, Museo Nazionale di S. Matteo. *Signed.*

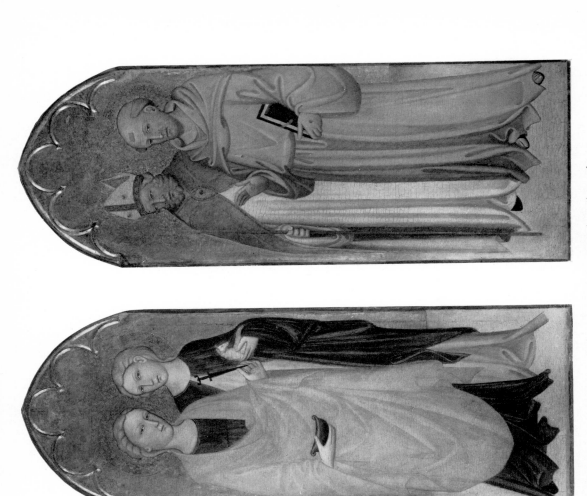

464. TURINO VANNI: *Altarpiece: Madonna and Child enthroned with six Angels. Paris, Louvre. Signed. Early work.*

465-6. TURINO VANNI: *Side-panels of polyptych: SS. Lucy and Agnes; Bishop Saint and S. Francis. Birmingham, Ala., Museum of Art, Kress Collection.*

468. TURINO VANNI: *Altarpiece: Madonna and Child enthroned, with three Archangels, three Angels, SS. John Baptist, John Evangelist, Peter, Anthony Abbot, Mary Magdalen, Catherine, Ursula and Lucy. Palermo, Galleria Nazionale. Signed and formerly dated. Late work.*

467. TURINO VANNI: *Altarpiece: Madonna and Child enthroned with SS. Ranieri and Torpè and two female Blessed. Pisa, S. Paolo a Ripa d'Arno. Signed and dated 1397.*

469. TADDEO DI BARTOLO: *Polyptych: Madonna and Child, SS. Sebastian, Paul, John Baptist and Nicholas.*
Formerly Collegalli, SS. Vito e Modesto. *Signed and dated 1389.*

470. TADDEO DI BARTOLO: *Madonna and Child with goldfinch*. **Detail**. Colle Val d'Elsa, S. Agostino.

471. TADDEO DI BARTOLO: *Centre panel of polyptych Madonna del Latte crowned by two Angels.* Budapest, Museum of Fine Arts.

472. TADDEO DI BARTOLO: *Processional standard: S. Donnino enthroned*. Pisa, Museo Nazionale di S. Matteo.

473. TADDEO DI BARTOLO: *Detail from the polyptych of the Assumption*. Montepulciano, Duomo. *1401*.

474. TADDEO DI BARTOLO: *Angel and Virgin of the Annunciation*. Bergen, Gallery. *Early work*.

475. TADDEO DI BARTOLO: *Detail from the polyptych of the Assumption: Self-portrait as S. Taddeus.*
Montepulciano, Duomo. *1401.*

476. TADDEO DI BARTOLO: *Predella panel: Scene from the life of S. Francis: Christmas Mass at Greccio.*
Hanover, Landesgalerie. *1403.*

477. TADDEO DI BARTOLO: *Detail from predella: Christ and Apostles.* New York, H. L. Moses.

478. TADDEO DI BARTOLO: *Polyptych: Madonna and Child; SS. Anthony Abbot, John Baptist, Michael, and Francis; in pinnacles, Redeemer and Angel and Virgin of the Annunciation; in roundels and pillars, six small Saints; in predella, five scenes. Volterra, Palazzo dei Priori. Signed and dated 1411.*

479. TADDEO DI BARTOLO: *Fresco: Apollo and Pallas, part of map of Rome.* Siena, Palazzo Pubblico, Anticappella. *1414.*

480. GREGORIO DI CECCO DI LUCA: *Centre panel of polyptych: Madonna of Humility suckling the Child, with six music-making Angels.* Siena, Opera del Duomo. *Signed and dated 1423.*

481. GIOVANNI DA PISA: *Triptych: Madonna and Child, S. John Baptist, S. Anthony Abbot; in pinnacles, Crucifixion, Angel and Virgin of the Annunciation; in pillars of frame, six Saints. San Simeon (Cal.), Hearst Memorial. Signed and dated 1423.*

482–3. GREGORIO DI CECCO DI LUCA: *Two predella panels: Birth of the Virgin. Rome, Vatican.—Marriage of the Virgin. London, National Gallery.*

484. GIOVANNI DA PISA: *Polyptych: Madonna enthroned; SS. Agatha and Stephen, SS. Francis and (?)Cristina; in roundels, two Prophets; in pinnacles, Crucifixion, Angel and Virgin of the Annunciation; in pillars of frame, six Saints; in predella, five stories from the life of S. Stephen. Detail. Formerly Rome, Cardinal Zelada. Signed.*

485. NICCOLÒ DI NALDO: *Detail of fresco: S. Ambrose*. Siena, Duomo, Sacristy. *1410*.

486. NICCOLÒ DI NALDO: *Detail of fresco: Defeated heretic*. Siena, Duomo, Sacristy. *1410*.

487. Benedetto di Bindo: *Detail of cupboard door: Judas before S. Helena.* Siena, Opera del Duomo.
1412–13.

488. GUALTIERI DI GIOVANNI DA PISA: *Fresco: Marriage of the Virgin*. Detail.
Siena, Duomo, Sacristy. *1411*.

489. GUALTIERI DI GIOVANNI DA PISA: *Fresco: The Virgin returning to her Parents*. Detail.
Siena, Duomo, Sacristy. *1411*.

490. GUALTIERI DI GIOVANNI DA PISA: *Triptych: Madonna and Child enthroned; S. Andrew, S. Onophrius.*
Siena, Pinacoteca.

491. GUALTIERI DI GIOVANNI DA PISA:
Fresco: Birth of the Virgin. Detail.
Siena, Duomo, Sacristy. *1411.*

492. GUALTIERI DI GIOVANNI DA PISA:
Madonna and Child enthroned, worshipped by kneeling monk.
Philadelphia, Fleischer Memorial.

493. Gualtieri di Giovanni da Pisa: *Madonna and Child.*
Notre Dame, Ind., University Art Gallery,
Kress Collection.

494. Gualtieri di Giovanni da Pisa:
Fresco: The Virgin returning to her parents.
Detail. Siena, Duomo, Sacristy. *1411.*

495. Gualtieri di Giovanni da Pisa: *Predella panel: S. Margaret meets Olibrius.* Berlin–Dahlem,
Staatliche Museen.

495a. *Sienese Book cover*. Siena, Archivio di Stato. *1377*.

THE LATE GOTHIC PERIOD

496. SALIMBENI: *Portable triptych: Mystic Marriage of S. Catherine; in wings, S. Simeon and S. Taddeus.* San Severino Marche, Pinacoteca. *Signed and dated 1400.*

497. SALIMBENI: *Votive fresco: Trinity.*
San Severino Marche, S. Lorenzo in Doliolo.

498. SALIMBENI: *Fragment of votive fresco: Apostle.*
Detail. San Severino Marche, S. Maria della Pieve.

499. SALIMBENI: *Votive fresco: Madonna and Child with Angel.*
Detail. San Severino Marche, S. Maria della Pieve.

500. SALIMBENI: *Fresco: The Virgin greeting Zacharias*. Detail. Urbino, Oratorio di S. Giovanni Battista. *Signed by Lorenzo and Jacopo and dated 1416.*

501. SALIMBENI: *Fresco: Annunciation to Zacharias, and Zacharias writing to S. Elizabeth*. Urbino, Oratorio di S. Giovanni Battista. *Signed and dated 1416.*

502. SALIMBENI: *Frescoed walls. Urbino, Oratorio di S. Giovanni Battista. Signed by Lorenzo and Jacopo, and dated 1416.*

503. SALIMBENI: *Fresco: Crucifixion.* Detail. Urbino, Oratorio di S. Giovanni Battista. *Signed and dated 1416.*

504. SALIMBENI: *Fresco: Baptism of Christ*. Detail. Urbino, Oratorio di S. Giovanni Battista.
Signed and dated 1416.

505. SALIMBENI: *Fresco: S. John Baptist preaching*. Detail. Urbino, Oratorio di S. Giovanni Battista.
Signed and dated 1416.

506. SALIMBENI: *Fresco: Baptism of the multitudes.* Detail. Urbino, Oratorio di S. Giovanni Battista.
Signed by Lorenzo and Jacopo and dated 1416.

507. SALIMBENI: *Fresco: Baptism of the multitudes*. Detail. Urbino, Oratorio di S. Giovanni Battista.
Signed by Lorenzo and Jacopo and dated 1416.

508. SALIMBENI: *Fresco: S. John Evangelist blames the philosopher Crato for advising two youths to break up their diamonds*. Detail. San Severino Marche, S. Severino (Duomo Vecchio).

509. SALIMBENI: *Fresco: S. John Evangelist distributes coins to the poor*. Detail. San Severino Marche, S. Severino (Duomo Vecchio.)

510. OTTAVIANO NELLI: *Polyptych: Madonna and Child with lily, and Trinity in pinnacle; SS. Anthony Abbot, Nicholas, Paul and Catherine; in pilasters, six small Saints.* Perugia, Galleria Nazionale dell'Umbria. *Signed and dated 1403.*

511. OTTAVIANO NELLI: *Dossal: Nativity, Madonna and Child with SS. John Baptist and Jerome and donors, Agony in the Garden.* Homeless.

512. OTTAVIANO NELLI: *Madonna of Humility with music-making Angels*. Homeless.

513. OTTAVIANO NELLI: *Fresco: Coronation of the Virgin*. Detail. Gubbio, S. Francesco.

514. OTTAVIANO NELLI: *Fresco: Convocation of the Virgin's suitors*. Gubbio, S. Francesco.

515. OTTAVIANO NELLI: *Frescoed apse*. Gubbio, S. Francesco.

516. OTTAVIANO NELLI: *Fresco: Annunciation to Joachim.* Gubbio, S. Francesco.

517. OTTAVIANO NELLI: *Side-panel of polyptych: Marriage of S. Francis with Poverty.*
Rome, Vatican, Pinacoteca.

518. OTTAVIANO NELLI: *Centre panel of polyptych: Adoration of the Magi.*
Worcester, Mass., Art Museum.

519. OTTAVIANO NELLI: *Fresco: Birth of the Virgin*. Foligno, Palazzo Trinci.

520. OTTAVIANO NELLI: *Fresco: Nativity*. Foligno, Palazzo Trinci.

521. OTTAVIANO NELLI: *Frescoes: Scenes from the life of S. Augustine*. Gubbio, S. Agostino.

522. RANUCCIO D'ARVARO: *Madonna suckling the Child, with kneeling Dominican and, above, two Prophets.* Legnago, Chiesa della Disciplina. *Signed.*

523. PIETRO DI DOMENICO DA MONTEPULCIANO:
Madonna of Humility with four Angels. New York,
Metropolitan Museum. *Signed and dated 1420.*

524. PIETRO DI DOMENICO DA MONTEPULCIANO:
Centre of polyptych: Madonna of Humility.
Osimo, Baptistery. *Dated 1418.*

525–7. PIETRO DI DOMENICO DA MONTEPULCIANO: *SS. Lawrence, Stephen, Michael and Cosmas.*
Altidona, Parish Church.

528. GENTILE DA FABRIANO: *Madonna and Child with S. Nicholas, S. Catherine and donor.*
Berlin-Dahlem, Staatliche Museen. *Signed. Early work.*

529. GENTILE DA FABRIANO: *Detail of polyptych: Coronation of the Virgin.*
Milan, Brera. *Signed. Early work.*

530. GENTILE DA FABRIANO: *Adoration of the Magi*. Detail. Florence, Uffizi. *Signed and dated 1423.*

532. GENTILE DA FABRIANO: *Madonna and Child enthroned with SS. Lawrence and Julian.* New York, Frick Collection.

531. GENTILE DA FABRIANO: *Coronation of the Virgin.* Paris, Heugel Collection.

533. GENTILE DA FABRIANO: *Reconstruction of Quaratesi polyptych: Madonna and Child enthroned with six Angels; in pinnacle, blessing Christ.* Hampton Court, Royal Collection.—SS. *Mary Magdalen, Nicholas, John Baptist and George; in pinnacles, Angel and Virgin of the Annunciation.* SS. *Francis and Dominic.* Florence, Uffizi.—*Predella: Scenes from the life of S. Nicholas of Bari.* Rome, Vatican, and Washington, National Gallery of Art, Kress Collection. 1425.

535. Michelino da Besozzo: *Mystic Marriage of S. Catherine.* Siena, Pinacoteca. *Signed.*

534. North Italian, close to Gentile da Fabriano: *Madonna and Child in glory worshipped by SS. Francis and Clare.* Pavia, Museo.

537. STEFANO DA ZEVIO: *Madonna and Child with God the Father and Angels in rose garden.* Worcester, Mass., Museum of Art.

536. STEFANO DA ZEVIO: *Madonna and Child with Angels.* Rome, Palazzo Colonna.

538. STEFANO DA ZEVIO: *Adoration of the Magi*. Milan, Brera. *Signed and dated 1435.*

539–40. NORTH ITALIAN CLOSE TO GENTILE DA FABRIANO AND STEFANO DA ZEVIO: *Frescoes:*
Young Hermit Saint; Angel. Pordenone, Duomo.

541–2. NORTH ITALIAN CLOSE TO GENTILE DA FABRIANO AND STEFANO DA ZEVIO: *Panels of polyptych:*
S. Benedict and the broken sieve; Florence, Uffizi.—*S. Benedict in the wilderness.* Milan, Museo Poldi-Pezzoli.

543. PISANELLO: *Madonna and Child with two small Saints in a pergola.*
Homeless. *Signed.*

544. PISANELLO: *Fresco around tomb of Niccolò Brenzoni: Annunciation.* Details. Verona, S. Fermo Maggiore.
Signed. 1426.

545. PISANELLO: *Profile of Ginevra d'Este* (?). Paris, Louvre. *Before 1438.*

546. PISANELLO: *Medal of Lionello d'Este*, obverse and reverse. *1444.* Milan, Medagliere municipale.

547. ZAVATTARI: *Detail of fresco: Banquet.* Monza, Duomo. *Signed and dated 1444.*

548. NORTH ITALIAN CLOSE TO PISANELLO: *Cassone panel: Story of S. Giovanni Boccadoro.* Modena, Galleria Estens

549. ZAVATTARI: *Fresco: Queen Teodolinda surveys the artists.* Monza, Duomo. *Signed and dated 1444.*

550. SASSETTA: *Predella panel: S. Thomas Aquinas praying in church.*
Budapest, Museum of Fine Arts. *1423–6*

551. SASSETTA: *The Journey of the Magi*. Fragment. New York, Metropolitan Museum.

552. SASSETTA: *Adoration of the Magi*. Fragment. Siena, Palazzo Chigi Saracini.

553. SASSETTA: *Madonna of Humility crowned by Angels*. New York, Miss Helen Frick.

554. SASSETTA: *Detail of polyptych: Madonna of the Snow crowned by two Angels.* Florence, Contini Bonacossi Collection. *Signed. 1430-2.*

555. SASSETTA: *Detail of the polyptych of the Madonna of the Snow: S. Paul, S. Francis, and Angel making snow-ball.* Florence, Contini Bonacossi Collection. *Signed. 1430-2.*

556. SASSETTA: *Reconstruction of polyptych from Borgo San Sepolcro, front, middle register: Madonna and Child enthroned with Angels, S. John Evangelist, S. Anthony of Padua.*
Paris, Louvre.—The Blessed Ranieri, S. John Baptist. Florence, Berenson Collection. 1437–44.

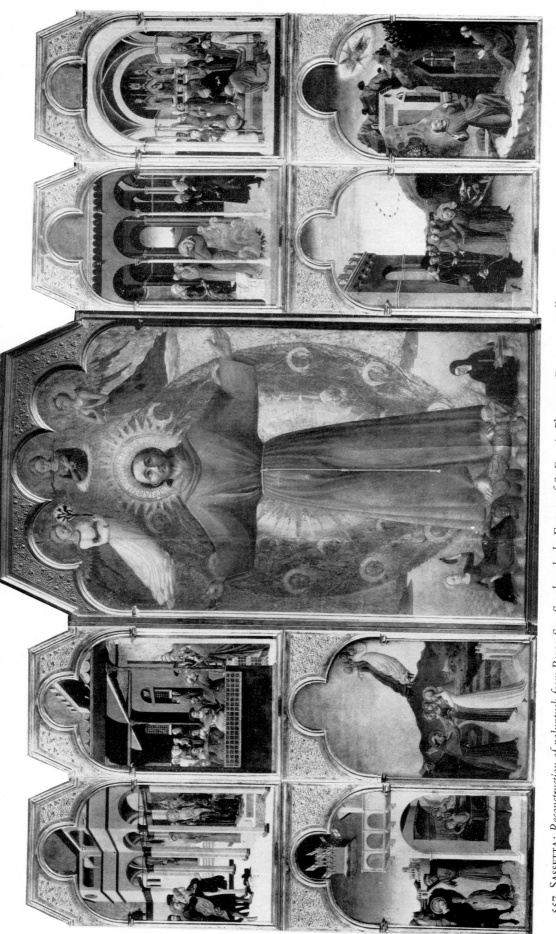

557. SASSETTA: *Reconstruction of polyptych from Borgo San Sepolcro, back: Ecstasy of S. Francis. Florence, Berenson Collection.—Mystic Marriage of S. Francis with Poverty. Chantilly, Musée Condé.—Seven other scenes from the life of S. Francis. London, National Gallery. 1437–44.*

558. SASSETTA: *Fresco: Coronation of the Virgin*. Detail. Siena, Porta Romana. *Begun 1447, left unfinished at artist's death.*

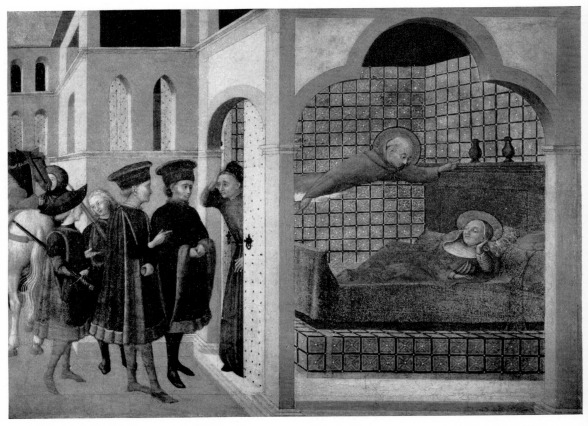

559. SASSETTA: *Predella panel: The Blessed Ranieri appears to a sleeping Cardinal*. Berlin-Dahlem, Staatliche Museen. *1437-44.*

560. AMBROSI: *Triptych of Nativity.* Detail. Asciano, Museo d'Arte Sacra. *About 1455.*

561. AMBROSI: *Predella panel: Miraculous birth of S. Nicholas.* Basel, Kunstmuseum. *About 1435.*

564. WORKSHOP OF SASSETTA: *Madonna and Child with two female Saints and two Angels; Crucifixion above. Homeless.*

563. AMBROSI: *Christ on the Cross. Venice, Conte Cini.*

562. AMBROSI: *Centre panel of portable altarpiece: Madonna and Child with Saints and Angels; Crucifixion above. Homeless.*

565–6. AMBROSI: *Two details from the triptych of the Nativity. Asciano, Museo d'Arte Sacra. About 1455.*

567. AMBROSI: *S. Augustine. Detail from the triptych of the Nativity.* Asciano, Museo d'Arte Sacra. *About 1455.*

568. AMBROSI: *Head of the Virgin.* Fragment. Esztergom, Museum.

569. AMBROSI: *Left panel of polyptych: S. Augustine.* Altenburg, Lindenau Museum.

570. AMBROSI: *Centre panel of triptych: Madonna and Child.* Brooklyn, N.Y., Museum.

571. AMBROSI: *Front of banner: Crucifixion with Flagellants*. Paris, Musée Jacquemart-André.
Signed and dated 1444.

572. AMBROSI: *S. Bernardino trampling on mitres.* Lucignano, Museo Civico.
Signed and dated 1448.

573. MASTER OF THE OSSERVANZA TRIPTYCH: *Triptych: Madonna and Child enthroned, with Angel and Virgin of the Annunciation in roundels above; SS. Ambrose and Jerome; in pinnacles, Redeemer, SS. Peter and Paul.* Siena, Osservanza. *Dated 1436.*

574. MASTER OF THE OSSERVANZA TRIPTYCH: *Detail from the polyptych of the Birth of the Virgin.*
Asciano, Museo d'Arte Sacra.

575. MASTER OF THE OSSERVANZA TRIPTYCH: *Detail from the polyptych of the Birth of the Virgin.*
Asciano, Museo d'Arte Sacra.

576. MASTER OF THE OSSERVANZA TRIPTYCH: *Portable altarpiece: Madonna of Humility with four Angels and blessing Redeemer; in wings, S. Francis and S. John Baptist, Angel and Virgin of the Annunciation.* Siena, Palazzo Chigi Saracini.

577. MASTER OF THE OSSERVANZA TRIPTYCH: *Predella panel: Crucifixion.* Kiev, Museum.

578. MASTER OF THE OSSERVANZA TRIPTYCH: *Predella panel: Christ on the way to Calvary.*
Philadelphia, John G. Johnson Collection.

579. MASTER OF THE OSSERVANZA TRIPTYCH: *Predella panel: Flagellation.*
Rome, Vatican Pinacoteca.

580. SANO DI PIETRO: *Madonna and Child with SS. Peter and Paul and four Angels.* Florence, Acton Collection.

581. SANO DI PIETRO: *Madonna and Child with SS. Jerome and Bernardino and four Angels.* Homeless.

582. SANO DI PIETRO: *Predella panel: While S. Augustine writes to S. Jerome, unaware of the latter's death, Jerome appears to him with S. John Baptist, who wears a triple tiara.* Paris, Louvre. *1444.*

583. SANO DI PIETRO: *S. Bernardino preaching in Piazza del Campo*. Siena, S. Maria Assunta.

584. SANO DI PIETRO: *Centre panel of polyptych: Madonna and Child, and S. Francis above.*
Montemerano, S. Giorgio. *Signed and dated 1458.*

585. SANO DI PIETRO: *The Virgin commanding Pope Callistus III to protect Siena.* Siena, Pinacoteca.
Signed and dated 1456.

586. Sano di Pietro: *Miniature: The Calling of the Sons of Zebedee.*
Siena, Piccolomini Library, Graduale no. 11.

587. Sano di Pietro: *Predella panel of the polyptych from S. Petronilla: S. Peter heals his paralytic daughter Petronilla. Siena, Pinacoteca. Dated 1479.*

588. SANO DI PIETRO: *Polyptych: Madonna and Child enthroned with two Benedictines, SS. Benedict and Cyrinus, SS. Donatus and Justina; above, Blessing Christ, Angel and Virgin of the Annunciation; in pilasters, SS. Jerome, Eugene, Maurus, SS. Gregory, Anthony Abbot and Placidus; in predella, Dead Christ with mourning Virgin and S. John Evangelist, S. Benedict rescuing a monk from the devil, S. Cyrinus thrown into the river, S. Donatus and the dragon, Stabbing of S. Justina.* Badia a Isola, SS. Salvatore e Cirino. Signed and dated 1471.

589. GIOVANNI DI PAOLO: *Christus patiens, Christus triumphans.*
Siena, Pinacoteca. *Early work.*

590. GIOVANNI DI PAOLO: *Predella panel of Pecci polyptych: Way to Golgotha.*
Baltimore, Walters Art Gallery. *1426.*

591. GIOVANNI DI PAOLO: *Centre panel of Pecci polyptych: Madonna of the Rosary and Angels.*
Castelnuovo Berardenga, Prepositura. *Signed and dated 1426.*

592–3. GIOVANNI DI PAOLO: *Fragments of polyptych: S. Ursula.* Houston, Texas, Museum of Art.—
Madonna and Child. Siena, Pinacoteca.

594. GIOVANNI DI PAOLO: *Predella panel: Flight into Egypt.* Siena, Pinacoteca. *1436.*

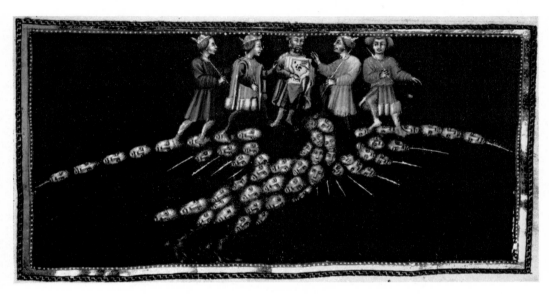

595–7. GIOVANNI DI PAOLO: *Miniatures from Dante codex: Beatrice explains the appearance of the moon; The five just princes; Folco inveighs against the corruption of the Florentines.* London, British Museum, Yates Thompson 36, fol. 132r., 164r., 145r.

598–600. GIOVANNI DI PAOLO: *S. Ambrose*. New York, Robert Lehman.—*S. Gregory*. Homeless.— *S. Augustine*. Cambridge, Mass., Fogg Art Museum.

601. GIOVANNI DI PAOLO: *Predella panel: Expulsion from Paradise*. New York, Robert Lehman. *1445*.

602. GIOVANNI DI PAOLO: *Beheading of S. John Baptist*. Chicago, Art Institute.

603. GIOVANNI DI PAOLO: *Crucifix*. Dublin, National Gallery of Ireland.

604. GIOVANNI DI PAOLO: *Detail from Crucifixion*. Siena, Pinacoteca. *Signed and dated 1440*.

605. GIOVANNI DI PAOLO:
Pilaster panel: S. Galganus.
Utrecht, Archiepiscopal Museum.

606. GIOVANNI DI PAOLO: *Madonna and Child.*
Tours, Musée.

607. GIOVANNI DI PAOLO: *Predella panel: S. Clare saves a child mauled by a wolf.* Houston, Texas,
Museum of Art.

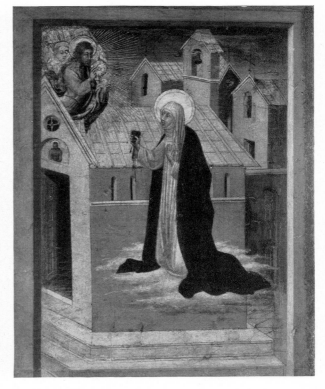

608–10. GIOVANNI DI PAOLO: *Three panels of polyptych: S. Catherine dictating to the Blessed Raimondo da Capua.*
Detroit, Art Institute.—*S. Catherine receiving stigmata.* New York, Robert Lehman.—
S. Catherine's Vision of Christ. Brussels, Michèle Stoclet. *1447–9.*

611. GIOVANNI DI PAOLO: *Predella panel: S. Nicholas of Tolentino appearing over the walls of a city hit by the plague.* Vienna, Academy.

612. GIOVANNI DI PAOLO: *Detail from the Last Judgement.* Siena, Pinacoteca.

613. GIOVANNI DI PAOLO: *Miniature: Death on Horseback*. Siena, Biblioteca Comunale, Antiphonal from Lecceto.

614. GIOVANNI DI PAOLO: *Predella panel: Christ and Saints*. Detail. Parma, Pinacoteca.

615. GIOVANNI DI PAOLO: *Fragmentary polyptych: Madonna and Child enthroned with four Angels, SS. Monica(?), Augustine, John Baptist and Nicholas of Tolentino.* New York, Metropolitan Museum, Signed and dated 1454.

616. GIACOMO DEL PISANO: *Madonna and Child with two Angels.* Richmond, Va., Museum of Art.

617. GIACOMO DEL PISANO: *Madonna adoring the Child and two Angels.* San Diego, Cal., Fine Arts Gallery.

18. GIACOMO DEL PISANO: *Triptych: Madonna and Child enthroned with two Angels; Penitent S. Mary Magdalen, S. Peter*. Dublin, National Gallery of Ireland. *Signed.*

618a. SASSETTA: *Vanity*. Detail from plate 557.

THE TRANSITION
FROM GOTHIC TO RENAISSANCE
IN CENTRAL ITALY

619–21. ANTONIO DA VITERBO THE ELDER: *Triptych: Christ enthroned; S. Peter, S. Paul.*
Capena, S. Michele. *Signed and dated 1451.*

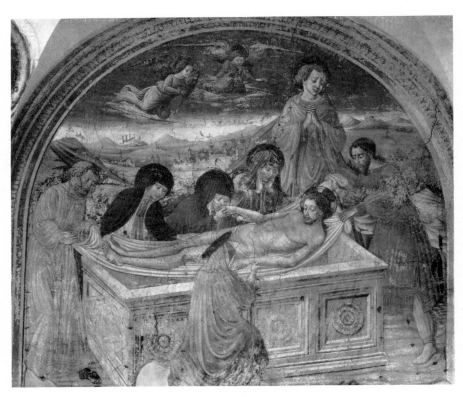

622. ANTONIO DA VITERBO THE ELDER: *Frescoed lunette: Entombment.*
Rome, Museo del Foro Romano.

623. Antonio da Viterbo the Elder: *Fresco: The Redeemer.*
Rome, Museo del Foro Romano.

624. Antonio da Viterbo the Elder: *Detail from fresco of the Crucifixion: SS. John the Evangelist and Francis.* Rome, Museo del Foro Romano.

625. BARTOLOMEO DI TOMMASO DA FOLIGNO: *Triptych: Coronation of the Virgin, Nativity, Adoration of the Magi.* Detail. Rome, Vatican Pinacoteca.

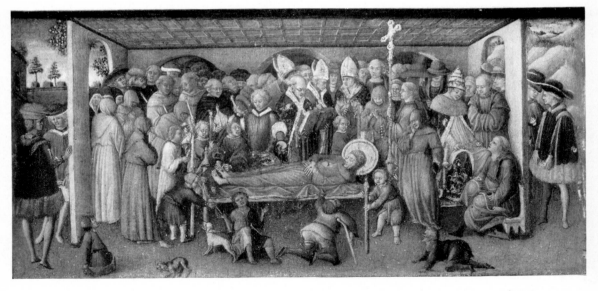

626. BARTOLOMEO DI TOMMASO DA FOLIGNO: *Predella panel: Funeral and Canonization of S. Francis.* Baltimore, Walters Art Gallery.

627. BARTOLOMEO DI TOMMASO DA FOLIGNO: *Predella panel: Agony in the Garden*. Detail.
Rome, Vatican Pinacoteca.

628. BARTOLOMEO DI TOMMASO DA FOLIGNO: *Predella panel: Lamentation and Entombment*.
New York, Metropolitan Museum.

629. Bartolomeo di Tommaso da Foligno: *Fragments of polyptych:*
Madonna and Child enthroned with six Angels and Rinaldo Trinci as donor;
S. John Baptist; the Blessed Pietro Crisci; in pinnacles, S. Bartholomew and S. Ursula.
Foligno, S. Salvatore. *1437.*

630. Bartolomeo di Tommaso da Foligno: *Predella panel: Entombment.* Homeless.

631. Bartolomeo di Tommaso da Foligno: *Fresco: The Descent of Christ into Limbo*. Terni, S. Francesco. *Formerly dated (1453?)*.

632. GIOVANNI FRANCESCO DA RIMINI: *Adoration of the Child with S. Helena and Infant S. John.*
Atlanta, Ga., Art Association Galleries, Kress Collection.

633. Giovanni Francesco da Rimini: *Triptych: Madonna and Child enthroned, S. Jerome, S. Francis.*
Perugia, Galleria Nazionale del'Umbria.

34. Giovanni Francesco da Rimini: *Madonna and Child and two heads of Angels.* London, National Gallery. *Signed and dated 1461.*

635. Giovanni Francesco da Rimini:
Madonna and Child with two Angels.
Homeless.

636. GIOVANNI FRANCESCO DA RIMINI: *Tondo: God the Father blessing and four Angels.*
Brooklyn, N.Y., Museum.

637. GIOVANNI FRANCESCO DA RIMINI: *Predella panel: S. Dominic fed by Angels.* Pesaro, Musei Civici.

638. Giovanni Francesco da Rimini and Matteo da Gualdo: *Triptych from S. Eufemia: Assumption, Bishop Saint, S. Lucy; in predella: S. Lucy helps the poor, is accused, stands fast against the oxen, Dead Christ in Tomb, two Angels.* Spoleto, Arcivescovado.

639. MATTEO DA GUALDO: *Madonna and Child enthroned, with SS. Francis, Bernardino, Margaret and Catherine*. Detail. Gualdo Tadino, Pinacoteca. *Signed and dated 1462.*

640. MATTEO DA GUALDO: *Votive fresco: S. Anne with Madonna and Child in her lap*. Sigillo, S. Maria della Scirca. *Signed and dated 1484.*

641. MATTEO DA GUALDO: *Madonna and Child enthroned in frame of carnations*. Baltimore, Walters Art Gallery.

642. Matteo da Gualdo: *Frescoed tabernacle: Madonna and Child enthroned with four Angels;*
in embrasure, God the Father blessing, S. Sebastian and S. Anthony Abbot.
Perugia, Galleria Nazionale dell'Umbria. *Signed and dated 1488.*

643. Matteo da Gualdo: Frescoes: Annunciation; below, imaginary Renaissance portico with putti throwing flowers and Angels holding candelabra;

644. MEZZASTRIS: *Frescoes: S. James saves from death by hanging the young pilgrim falsely accused of theft*. Assisi, Oratorio dei Pellegrini. *Signed. About 1468–70.*

645. MEZZASTRIS: *Frescoed lunette: Madonna and Child with Angels, SS. Lucy and Clare.*
Foligno, Monastero di S. Lucia. *Signed and dated 1471.*

646. MEZZASTRIS: *Fresco: S. Anthony Abbot blessing the camels.* Detail. Assisi, Oratorio dei Pellegrini.
About 1468–70.

647. MEZZASTRIS: *Detached fresco: Madonna and Child with two Angels,
SS. Francis and John Baptist. Detail. Foligno, Pinacoteca.
Signed and dated 1499.*

648. MEZZASTRIS: *Frescoed tabernacle: Madonna and Child with SS. John Evangelist and John Baptist, and
two Angels. Foligno, Maestà Bella. Signed.*

649. MEZZASTRIS: *Fresco: Crucifixion*. Foligno, S. Maria in Campis, Cappella di Cola delle Casse.
About 1456.

650. NICCOLÒ DA FOLIGNO: *Fragment of fresco: Crucifixion*. Foligno, S. Maria in Campis, Cappella di S. Marta. *1456*.

651–2. NICCOLÒ DA FOLIGNO: *Details of fresco round a carved crucifix: Mourning Virgin and S. John Evangelist*. Foligno, S. Feliciano.

653. NICCOLÒ DA FOLIGNO: *Centre panel of triptych: Madonna and Child with SS. Francis and Bernardino,
Angels and donor.* Deruta, Palazzo Comunale. *Signed and dated 1457.*

654. Niccolò da Foligno: *Plague banner from Assisi: The Virgin and SS. Sebastian, Clare, Francis, Rufinus, Victorinus and Roch implore Christ to save Assisi from the plague. Kevelaer, Presbytery. After 1460 and before 1472.*

655–6. NICCOLÒ DA FOLIGNO: *Front and back of processional standard: Madonna and S. Anne with Angels.* New York, Robert Lehman.—*S. Michael.* Princeton University Art Museum. *Early work.*

657. NICCOLÒ DA FOLIGNO: *Predella panel: Funeral of S. Rufinus.* Assisi, S. Ruffino. *Signed and dated 1460.*

658. NICCOLÒ DA FOLIGNO: *Polyptych: Nativity; above, Coronation; SS. Lawrence, Rinaldus, Felicissimus and Francis; SS. Sebastian, John Baptist, Paul and Catherine; Church Fathers; in pilasters, ten small Saints; in predella, Twelve Apostles, two Seraphim, two Angels with emblem of Nocera and coat of arms of Bishop Francesco Scelloni. Nocera Umbra, Pinacoteca. Signed and dated 1483.*

659. NICCOLÒ DA FOLIGNO: *Predella panels: Agony in the Garden, Flagellation*. Paris, Louvre. *Signed and dated 1492.*

660. NICCOLÒ DA FOLIGNO: *Predella panel: The Way to Calvary*. Paris, Louvre. *Signed and dated 1492.*

661. Niccolò da Foligno: *Centre panel of polyptych: Nativity*. Foligno, Pinacoteca. *1492*.

662–3. ANDREA DELITIO: *Diptych: Mystic Marriage of S. Catherine; Crucifixion.* Aquila, Museo Nazionale Abbruzzese.

664. ANDREA DELITIO: *Predella panel: S. Benedict blessing Totila.* Providence, Rhode Island School of Design.

665. ANDREA DELITIO: *Detail from portable triptych: Madonna and Child enthroned;
above, Christ on the Cross*. Baltimore, Walters Art Gallery.

666. ANDREA DELITIO: *Frescoes: Allegories of Charity and Justice; Meeting at the Golden Gate; Visitation; Nativity; Adoration of the Magi. Atri, S. Maria Assunta.*

667. ANDREA DELITIO: *Frescoes: Allegories of Prudence and Obedience; Expulsion of Joachim; Birth, Presentation and Education of the Virgin*. Atri, S. Maria Assunta.

668. ANDREA DELITIO: *Ceiling fresco: SS. Luke and Ambrose.* Atri, S. Maria Assunta.

669. ANDREA DELITIO: *Fresco: Flight into Egypt.* Atri, S. Maria Assunta.

670. ANDREA DELITIO: *Fresco: The Virgin receiving the annunciation of her death.* Detail. Atri, S. Maria Assunta.

671. ARCANGELO DI COLA DA CAMERINO: *Wing of diptych: Madonna and Child enthroned with six Angels*. New York, Miss Helen C. Frick. *Signed*.

672. ARCANGELO DI COLA DA CAMERINO: *Wing of diptych: Crucifixion.*
New York, Miss Helen C. Frick. *Signed.*

673. ARCANGELO DI COLA DA CAMERINO: *Portable altarpiece: Madonna and Child enthroned; S. Francis receiving stigmata; SS. Anthony Abbot and Bartholomew; Crucifixion; S. Christopher.* Detail. Venice, Conte Vittorio Cini.

674. ARCANGELO DI COLA DA CAMERINO: *Predella panel: Adoration of the Magi.* Philadelphia, John G. Johnson Collection.

675. ARCANGELO DI COLA DA CAMERINO: *Madonna and Child holding jasmin*. Bergen, Gallery.

676. CAPORALI: *Madonna and Child*. Homeless. *Early work*.

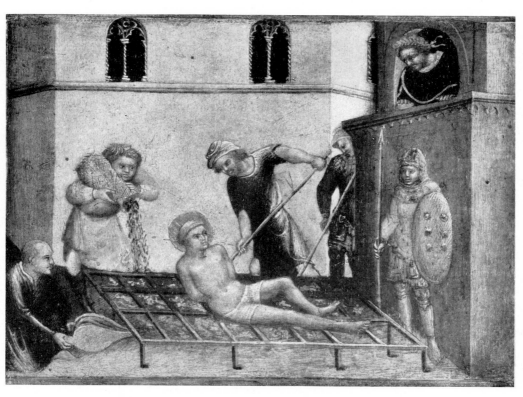

677. ARCANGELO DI COLA DA CAMERINO: *Predella panel: Martyrdom of S. Lawrence*. Venice, Conte Vittorio Cini.

678. CAPORALI: *Frescoed niche: Madonna and Child with six Angels.*
Deruta, La Fanciullata.

679. CAPORALI: *Predella panel: Adoration of the Magi and Christ on the Cross.* London, National Gallery.

680. CAPORALI: *Fresco: Madonna and Child in glory with SS. Anthony Abbot and Bernardino; below, SS. Sebastian and Roch plead for the Faithful; in embrasure, roundels with Christ, Prophets and Sibyls; on face of arch, God the Father, Angel and Virgin of the Annunciation.* Montelabbate, S. Maria. *Dated 1488.*

681–2. CAPORALI: *Two pinnacles of triptych: Angel and Virgin of the Annunciation.* Perugia, Galleria Nazionale dell'Umbria. *1467.*

683–4. BONFIGLI: *Two panels of triptych: Bishop Saint and S. Sebastian.* Homeless.—*Madonna of Humility.* El Paso, Texas, Museum of Art, Kress Collection.

685. BONFIGLI: *Detail from Annunciation with S. Luke.* Perugia, Galleria Nazionale dell'Umbria.

686. BONFIGLI: *Detail of processional banner: Madonna and Child in glory with Angels.*
Perugia, S. Fiorenzo. *Dated 1476.*

687. BONFIGLI: *Fresco: The body of S. Herculanus transferred to the Church of S. Lorenzo.* Perugia, Galleria Nazionale dell'Umbria. *Begun 1454 and not finished at the artist's death in 1496.*

THE EARLY RENAISSANCE

688. SQUARCIONE: *Madonna and Child*. Berlin-Dahlem, Staatliche Museen. *Signed*.

689. SQUARCIONE: *Polyptych: Penitent S. Jerome and SS. Lucy, John Baptist, Anthony Abbot and Justina.* Padua, Museo Civico. *Between 1449 and 1452.*

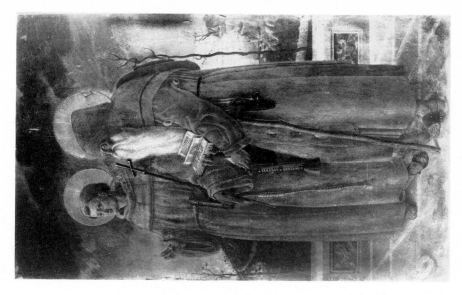

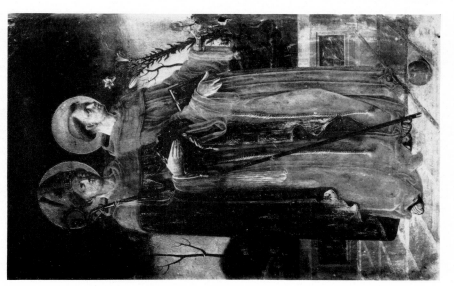

690. SCHIAVONE: *Triptych: Madonna and Child.* Berlin-Dahlem, Staatliche Museen. *Signed.*—SS. *Francis and Anthony Abbot, SS. Louis and Prosdocimus.* Padua, Duomo.

692. SCHIAVONE: *Madonna and Child with two music-making Angels*. Baltimore, Walters Art Gallery. *Signed*.

691. SCHIAVONE: *Madonna and Child with putti*. Turin, Galleria Sabauda. *Signed*.

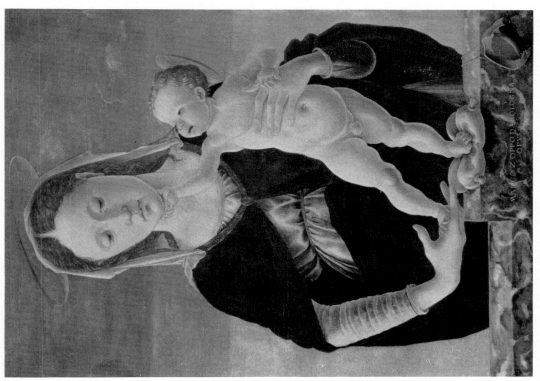

694. ZOPPO: *Madonna and Child.* Washington, National Gallery of Art,
Kress Collection. *Signed.*

693. ZOPPO: *Madonna suckling the Child, and Angels.* Canford Manor,
Viscount Wimbourne. *Signed. 1453–5.*

695–6. ZOPPO: *Two panels of polyptych:*
S. Augustine. London, National Gallery.—*S. Jerome.* Baltimore, Walters Art Gallery.

697. ZOPPO: *Predella panel: S. Francis receiving stigmata.* Baltimore, Walters Art Gallery.

698. Zoppo: *Detail of polyptych: SS. John Baptist and Jerome*. Bologna, Collegio di Spagna.

699. ZOPPO: *S. Jerome in the wilderness.* Lugano, Thyssen Collection. *Signed.*

700. ZOPPO: *Madonna and Child enthroned with SS. John Baptist, Francis, Paul and Jerome.*
Berlin-Ost, Staatliche Museen. *Signed and dated 1471.*

701. MANTEGNA: *Frescoed lunette: SS. Anthony of Padua and Bernardino kneeling.* Padua, Basilica del Santo.
Signed and dated 1452.

702. MANTEGNA: *Bust of S. Mark.* Frankfurt, Staedel Institute. *Signed. Early work.*

703. MANTEGNA: *S. Eufemia*. Naples, Museo del Capodimonte.
Signed and dated 1454.

704. MANTEGNA: *Fresco: S. James baptizing Hermogenes.* Formerly Padua, Eremitani. Destroyed.

705. MANTEGNA: *Wing of triptych: SS. Benedict, Lawrence, Zeno and John Baptist.*
Verona, S. Zeno. *1459.*

706. MANTEGNA: *Frescoed decoration. Mantua, Palazzo Ducale, Camera degli Sposi. Signed and dated 1474.*

707. MANTEGNA: *Allegory of Vice and Virtue*, from the Palazzo Ducale in Mantua. Paris, Louvre. *Late work.*

708. MANTEGNA: *Cartoon for lost fresco: Triumph of Caesar*. Hampton Court, Royal Collection. *1484–92*.

709. **Mantegna**: *Cartoon for lost fresco: Triumph of Caesar*. Hampton Court, Royal Collection. *1484-92*.

710. MANTEGNA: *Adoration of the Magi*. Castle Ashby, Marquess of Northampton. *Late work*.

711. STUDIO OF MANTEGNA: *Panel with Tritons and Satyrs*. Detail. Formerly Carpi, Foresti Collection.

712. MANTEGNA: *S. Sebastian*. Venice, Ca'd'Oro. *Late work*.

713. PARENTINO: *Minstrels performing*. Berlin-Dahlem, Staatliche Museen.

714. PARENTINO: *S. Louis of France distributing alms*. Rome, Galleria Doria Pamphili.

715. PARENTINO: *Christ carrying the Cross, with SS. Jerome and Augustine*. Modena, Galleria Estense. *Signed*.

716. PARENTINO: *The Temptations of S. Anthony Abbot*. Rome, Galleria Doria Pamphili.

717. PARENTINO: *Fresco from S. Giustina, Padua: Battle scene*. Pavia, Museo Malaspina.

718. PARENTINO: *Saint performing miracles*. Venice, Conte Cini.

719. Parentino(?): *Adoration of the Magi*. Detail. Homeless.

720. Parentino: *Story of Jason(?)*. Formerly Vienna, Emile Weinberger.

721. MICHELE PANNONIO: *Allegorical figure of Summer*. Budapest, Museum. *Signed*.

722. Tura: *'Primavera'*. London, National Gallery.

723. TURA: *Detail of organ-shutter: Angel of the Annunciation.*
Ferrara, Museo dell'Opera del Duomo. *1468–9.*

724. TURA: *Flight into Egypt*. New York, Metropolitan Museum.

725. TURA: *Lunette to Roverella altarpiece: Pietà.* Paris, Louvre.

726–7. TURA: *S. George and the Dragon.* Venice, Conte Cini.—*S. Maurelius.* Milan, Museo Poldi Pezzoli.

728. TURA: *S. Maurelius before the Judge.* Ferrara, Pinacoteca.

729. BALDASSARE D'ESTE: *Francesco Gonzaga as a boy*.
Washington, National Gallery of Art, Kress Collection.

730. BALDASSARE D'ESTE: *Tito Strozzi(?)*.
Venice, Conte Cini. *Signed and dated 1493.*

731. BALDASSARE D'ESTE AND COSSA: *Borso d'Este and his courtiers*. Detail of plate 732.

732. COSSA: *Fresco: The Month of March*. Ferrara, Palazzo Schifanoia, Sala dei Mesi, East wall. *1470*.

733. Cossa: *Stained glass window: Madonna and Child enthroned*. Berlin-Koepenick,
Kunstgewerbemuseum. *1462–7*.

734. COSSA: *Annunciation*. Dresden, Gallery. *About 1470–2.*

735. COSSA: *Ladies at work*. Detail of plate 732.

736. COSSA: *A hunter*. Detail of plate 732.

738. COSSA: *Side-panel of Griffoni polyptych: S. Lucy.* Washington,
National Gallery of Art. Kress Collection.

737. COSSA: *Detail of the Pala del Foro dei Mercanti: S. Petronius.*
Bologna, Pinacoteca. *Signed and dated 1474.*

739. FERRARESE, BEFORE 1510: *Cassone panel: Susanna and the Elders. Formerly Paris, Van Moppes Collection.*

740. FERRARESE, BEFORE 1510: *Cassone panel: Punishment of the Elders. Formerly London, Forbes Collection.*

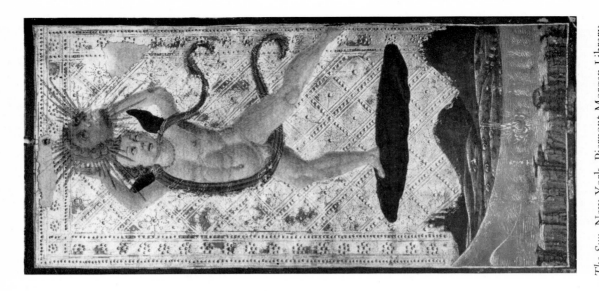

741–3. CICOGNARA: *Three Tarocchi cards: The castle of Pluto; Lady with star.* Bergamo, Accademia Carrara.—*The Sun.* New York, Pierpont Morgan Library. About 1480.

745. FERRARESE, BEFORE 1510: *Uberto de' Sacrati with his wife and son.* Munich, Alte Pinakothek.

744. CICOGNARA: *Madonna and Child in niche.* Ferrara, Pinacoteca, Berenson Gift. *Signed and dated 1480.*

746. FERRARESE, BEFORE 1510: *Madonna and Child enthroned with two Angels.* Homeless.
747. FERRARESE, BEFORE 1510. *Madonna and Child enthroned.* Bologna, Pinacoteca.

748. FERRARESE, BEFORE 1510: *Fresco: The Month of July.* Detail. Ferrara, Palazzo Schifanoia, Sala dei Mesi, North wall. *1470.*

749. ERCOLE DA FERRARA: *Madonna and Child enthroned with SS. Anne, Elizabeth, Augustine and Blessed Pietro degli Onesti*. Milan, Brera. *1480–1*.

750. ERCOLE DA FERRARA: *Predella panel: Pietà*. Liverpool, Walker Art Gallery.
Before 1486.

751. ERCOLE DA FERRARA: *Abraham and Melchizedek*. Detail. Old copy. Formerly Rome, Principe Chigi.

752. ERCOLE DA FERRARA: *Nativity*. London, National Gallery.

753. ERCOLE DA FERRARA: *The Gathering of Manna*. Detail. London, National Gallery.

754. FRANCESCO BIANCHI FERRARI: *Madonna and Child enthroned with SS. Francis, John Baptist, Ambrose and Jerome*. Berlin-East, Staatliche Museen. *Signed.*

755. FRANCESCO BIANCHI FERRARI: *Crucifixion with SS. Jerome and Francis*. Modena, Galleria Estense.

757. FRANCESCO BIANCHI FERRARI: *Crucifixion with SS. Dominic and Peter Martyr. Formerly Rome, Jannetti Del Grande.*

756. FRANCESCO BIANCHI FERRARI: *Madonna and Child enthroned with SS. Sebastian and Jerome and three music-making Angels. Modena, S. Pietro. Late work.*

758–9. Francesco Bianchi Ferrari: *Details of predella: Scenes from the life of S. Jerome.* Modena, S. Pietro. *Late work.*

PIERO DELLA FRANCESCA
AND THE SCHOOL OF CAMERINO

759a. PIERO DELLA FRANCESCA: *Fresco: Sigismondo Malatesta and his Patron Saint*. Detail.
Rimini, S. Francesco. *Signed and dated 1451.*

760. PIERO DELLA FRANCESCA: *Detail of fresco: S. Sigismund*. Rimini, S. Francesco. *Signed and dated 1451.*

761. PIERO DELLA FRANCESCA: *Detail of polyptych: Madonna of Mercy*. San Sepolcro, Pinacoteca.
Commissioned 1445.

762. PIERO DELLA FRANCESCA: *Architectural view*. Urbino, Galleria Nazionale delle Marche.

763. PIERO DELLA FRANCESCA: *Detail of fresco: The Victory of Heraclius.* Arezzo, San Francesco. *1452–66.*

764. PIERO DELLA FRANCESCA: *Madonna and Child enthroned with four Angels, SS. John Baptist, Bernardino,
Jerome, Francis, Peter Martyr, John Evangelist, and kneeling Federigo da Montefeltro.* Milan, Brera.
Probably about 1469–73.

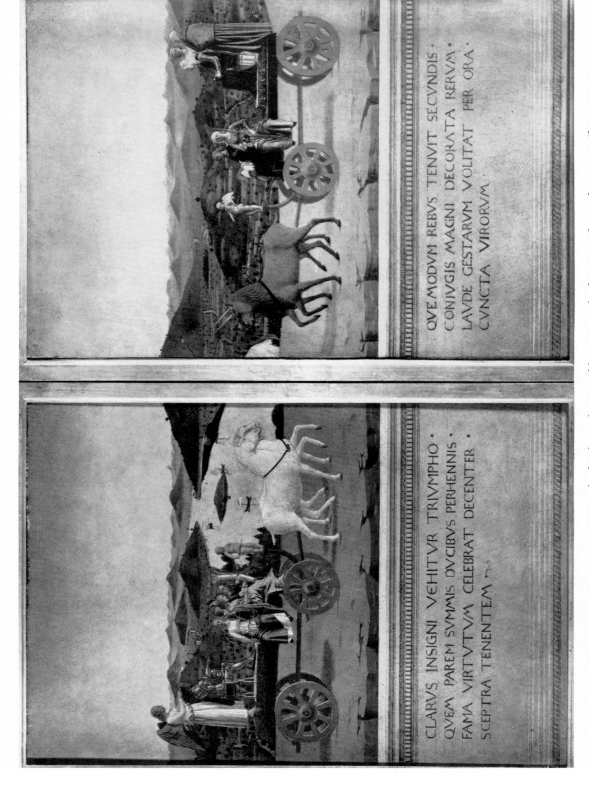

765. PIERO DELLA FRANCESCA: *Triumph of Federigo da Montefeltro; Triumph of Battista Sforza.* Florence, Uffizi. 1465–6.

767. Studio of Piero della Francesca: *Madonna and Child enthroned with four Angels.* Williamstown, Mass., Clark Art Institute.

766. Piero della Francesca: *S. Jerome with kneeling Girolamo Amadi.* Venice, Accademia. Signed.

768. PIERO DELLA FRANCESCA: *Panel from polyptych: S. Michael.*
London, National Gallery.

769. BOCCATI: *Madonna and Child enthroned with eight Angels and four putti*. Ajaccio, Musée Fesch.

770. BOCCATI: '*Madonna del Pergolato*' *with Angels and Saints*. Detail. Perugia, Galleria Nazionale
dell'Umbria. *Signed and dated 1447.*

771. BOCCATI: *Predella panel of the 'Madonna del Pergolato': Way to Calvary*. Perugia,
Galleria Nazionale dell'Umbria. *1447.*

772. Boccati: *Madonna and Child enthroned with six Angels*. Formerly Rome, Nevin Collection.

773. Boccati: *Centre panel of triptych: 'Madonna delle Lacrime'*. Seppio, S. Maria. *Dated 1466.*

774. Boccati: *Predella panel of the 'Madonna del Pergolato': Crucifixion*. Perugia, Galleria Nazionale dell'Umbria. *1447.*

775. BOCCATI: *Polyptych*. Belforte sul Chienti, S. Eustachio. *Signed and dated 1468.*

776. BOCCATI: *Madonna and sleeping Child with four putti.*
Palermo, Chiaramonte Bordonaro Collection.

777. BOCCATI: *Predella panel: Banquet of Totila and S. Savinus.* Formerly London, Sir Thomas Barlow.
Probably 1473.

778. GIROLAMO DI GIOVANNI DA CAMERINO: *Pinnacles: Angel and Virgin of the Annunciation*
Formerly Rome, Del Pero Collection.

779. GIROLAMO DI GIOVANNI DA CAMERINO: *Lower register of polyptych from Gualdo Tadino: Madonna and Child enthroned with six Angels and SS. Nicholas, Catherine, Apollonia and Nicholas of Tolentino.* Milan, Brera.

780. Girolamo di Giovanni da Camerino: *Processional standard: Crucifixion.*
Sarnano, S. Maria di Piazza.

781. GIROLAMO DI GIOVANNI DA CAMERINO: *S. John Baptist
with kneeling donor*. Paris, Musées Nationaux.

782. GIROLAMO DI GIOVANNI DA CAMERINO: *Annunciation and donors; in lunette, Pietà with two Franciscan Saints, Angels, Symbols of the Passion and Self-portrait*. Camerino, Pinacoteca.

783. GIROLAMO DI GIOVANNI DA CAMERINO: *Detail of polyptych: Madonna and Child enthroned with four Angels.* Montesanmartino, S. Maria del Pozzo. *Signed and dated 1473.*

784. ANTONIO DA FABRIANO: *S. Jerome in his study*. Baltimore, Walters Art Gallery.
Signed and dated 1451.

785. ANTONIO DA FABRIANO: *Crucifix*. Matelica, Museo. *Signed and dated 1452.*

786. ANTONIO DA FABRIANO: *Death of the Virgin*. Fabriano, Museo.

787–8. ANTONIO DA FABRIANO: *Left panel of polyptych: S. Clement blessing*. Richmond, Virginia Museum of Art.—*Side-panels of polyptych: S. Mary Magdalen, S. Francis*. Details. Formerly Cerreto d'Esi, Parish Church.

789. ANTONIO DA FABRIANO: *Side-panels of triptych: S. Clement; S. John Baptist.*
Genga, S. Clemente. *Signed and dated 1474.*

790. ANTONIO DA FABRIANO: *Centre panel of triptych: Madonna and Child with Angels.*
Genga, S. Clemente. *Signed and dated 1474.*

790a. DOMENICO DI BARTOLO: *Detail of marble intarsia on his design: Emperor Sigismund enthroned.*
Siena, Duomo. *1434.*

791. DOMENICO DI BARTOLO: *Fragment of altarpiece: Madonna and Child enthroned*. Princeton, N.J., University Museum.

792. DOMENICO DI BARTOLO: *Madonna and Child*. Philadelphia, John G. Johnson Collection. *Signed and dated 1437*.

793. DOMENICO DI BARTOLO: *Cassone panel: A couple kneeling before a king*. Bridgeport, Conn., Museum of Art, Kress Collection.

794. Domenico di Bartolo: *Madonna and Child enthroned with SS. Peter and Paul*. Washington,
National Gallery of Art, Kress Collection.

795. DOMENICO DI BARTOLO: *Fresco: Marriage of Foundlings*. Siena, Spedale di S. Maria della Scala, Pellegrinaio. *1440*.

796. Domenico di Bartolo: *Fresco: Pope Celestinus III grants privilege of independence to the Spedale*. Detail.
Siena, Spedale della Scala, Pellegrinaio. *1443*.

797. VECCHIETTA: *Fresco: The Virgin receives the souls of the Foundlings ('La scala del Paradiso').* Siena,
Spedale di S. Maria della Scala, Pellegrinaio. *1441.*

798. Vᴇᴄᴄʜɪᴇᴛᴛᴀ: *Wooden pigmented statue of Risen Christ*. Detail. Vico Alto, Parish Church. *1442*.

799. VECCHIETTA: *Detail of 'arliquiera': S. Catherine of Siena in prayer*. Siena, Pinacoteca. *1445*.

800. VECCHIETTA: *Detail of fresco of Last Judgement: S. Michael.* Siena, Spedale di S. Maria della Scala, Sala di S. Pietro. *Signed and dated 1449.*

801. VECCHIETTA: *Frescoed vault: Four Articles of the Creed (One Holy Catholic Church, The Forgiveness of Sins, The Resurrection of the Body, The Communion of Saints).* Siena, Baptistery.

802. VECCHIETTA: *Fresco: The Way to Calvary*. Siena, Baptistery.

803. VECCHIETTA: *Triptych: Madonna and Child, SS. Bartholomew, James and kneeling Eligius, SS. Andrew, Lawrence and kneeling Dominic; four small Saints in pilasters.* Florence, Uffizi. *Signed and dated 1457.*

804. VECCHIETTA: *Predella panel: Martyrdom of S. Blaise.* Pienza, Museo Diocesano.

805. VECCHIETTA: *Centre panel of triptych: The Assumption.*
Pienza, Duomo. *Signed. 1461–2.*

EVSEITA

QVESTA · E · LENTRATA · DELLVENERABILE · ANGNIOLO · DIPIET
RO · DIBALDO · CHMARLENGO · ALTEIPO · DE SAVI HVOMINI · FILIP
O DIPIEROMIDI · BANTONIO · DABAGNIAIA · EPERO DIBARTLOME
O DICHARLO · ETOMASSO · DORBANO GIOVANNELI · ETOIASS
O DIMISERE GIORGIOTO · NASSI EANTONIO · DIGIOVANIPINI · EL
OTIO DICHELO · DERONDINA · EGIORGIO · DIFRANCIO · DACHAI
RIGI · ATLOMEI · E DOMENICO · DIVENTVRINO · VENTVRINI MCCCC 60

806. VECCHIETTA: *Book-cover: The Coronation of Pope Pius II. Siena, Archivio. Dated 1460.*

807. VECCHIETTA: *Bronze statue: The Risen Christ*. Detail. Siena, Spedale di S. Maria della Scala.
Signed and dated 1476.

808. MATTEO DI GIOVANNI: *Madonna and Child with SS. Jerome and Barbara.*
Ravenna, Pinacoteca.

809. MATTEO DI GIOVANNI: *Predella panel: The Marriage of the Virgin (with portraits of Alberti and Donatello).*
Philadelphia, John G. Johnson Collection. *Early work.*

810. MATTEO DI GIOVANNI: *Madonna and Child enthroned with six Angels and SS. Anthony of Padua and Bernardino*. Detail. Siena, Museo dell'Opera del Duomo. *Signed and dated 1460*.

811. MATTEO DI GIOVANNI: *S. Barbara enthroned with Angels and SS. Mary Magdalen and Catherine*. Detail. Siena, S. Domenico. *Signed and dated 1479.*

812. Matteo di Giovanni: *Madonna and Child enthroned with SS. Jerome, Augustine, Nicholas and Martin.*
Pienza, Duomo.

813. Matteo di Giovanni: *Predella panel: A Vision of S. Jerome.* Chicago, Art Institute. *14(82?).*

814. MATTEO DI GIOVANNI: *Marble intarsia: Massacre of the Innocents*. Siena, S. Maria Assunta. *1481*.

815–17. MATTEO DI GIOVANNI: *Reconstruction of lunette from S. Agostino, Siena: S. Augustine.* Formerly London, Viscount Allendale.—*Madonna and Child with two Angels.* Esztergom, Museum.—*S. Francis.* Milan, Saibene Collection. *14(82?).*

818. MATTEO DI GIOVANNI: *Massacre of the Innocents.* Naples, Galleria Nazionale. *14(8)8.*

819. MATTEO DI GIOVANNI: *Massacre of the Innocents*. Detail. Siena, S. Agostino. *Signed and dated 1482.*

820. MATTEO DI GIOVANNI: *Massacre of the Innocents*. Detail. Siena, S. Maria dei Servi.
Signed and dated 1491.

821. COZZARELLI: *Detail of predella panel: Scene from the life of S. Barbara.* Rome, Vatican Pinacoteca. *1479.*

822. COZZARELLI: *Detail of cassone front: The Return of Ulysses.* Paris, Musée de Cluny.

823. COZZARELLI: *Annunciation and Departure for Bethlehem*. Coral Gables, Fla., Lowe Art Gallery, Kress Collection.

824. COZZARELLI: *Fresco: Madonna and Child enthroned, crowned by Angels.*
Formerly Siena, Tabernacle in Piazza del Campo.

825. COZZARELLI: *Predella panel: Martyrdom of SS. Simon and Taddeus.* Rotterdam, Museum Boymans—
Van Beuningen. *1486.*

826. COZZARELLI: *Baptism of Christ with SS. Jerome and Augustine*. Sinalunga, S. Bernardino.

827. COZZARELLI: *Illuminated page with Isaac blessing Jacob*. Siena, S. Maria Assunta (Duomo),
Libreria Piccolomini.

828. COZZARELLI: *Book-cover: Measuring the corn*. Formerly Vienna, A. Figdor.

829. COZZARELLI: *Adoration of the Shepherds*. Homeless.

830. COZZARELLI: *Detail of predella: Dead Christ held by two Angels, with the Virgin and S. John Evangelist.*
London, Julia Strachey.

831. MASTER OF STRATONICE: *Madonna and Child with Saints and Angels*. Detail. Birmingham, Ala. Museum of Art, Kress Collection.

832. MASTER OF STRATONICE: *Madonna and Child with Angel*. Geneva, Lederer Collection.

833. MASTER OF STRATONICE: *Three Saints*. Homeless.

834. MASTER OF STRATONICE: *Rape of Proserpina*. Homeless.

835. MASTER OF STRATONICE: *Cassone panel: Illness of Antiochus and his doctor's talk with King Seleucus.*
San Marino, Cal., Huntington Museum.

836. MASTER OF STRATONICE: *Orpheus in Hades*. Homeless.

837. MASTER OF STRATONICE: *Cassone panel: Marriage of Antiochus and Stratonice*. San Marino, Cal., Huntington Museum.

838. ANDREA DI NICCOLÒ: *Mass of S. Gregory*. Formerly Paris, Léon Bonnat. *Early work*.

839. ANDREA DI NICCOLÒ: *Madonna and Child with SS. Bernardino, Peter, Sebastian and Louis of Toulouse;*
in lunette, Massacre of the Innocents; in predella, S. Bernardino rescues the drowning boy Carinus; Calling of
the Sons of Zebedee, Crucifixion, Martyrdom of S. Sebastian, Beheading of S. Sigismund. Casole, Collegiata.
Signed and dated 1498.

840. ANDREA DI NICCOLÒ: *Nativity and Saints.* Siena, Pinacoteca.

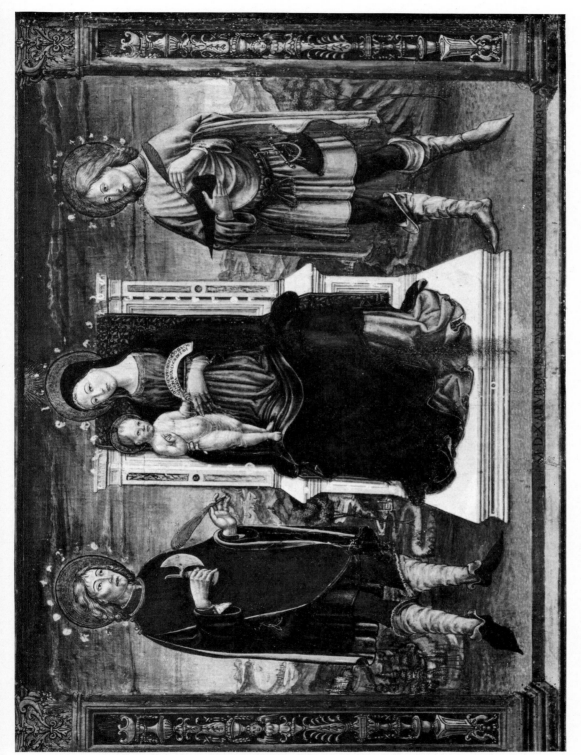

841. ANDREA DI NICCOLÒ: *Madonna and Child with SS. Crispin and Crispinianus.* Siena, S. Mustiola alla Rosa. *Dated 1510.*

842. BENVENUTO DI GIOVANNI: *Annunciation with SS. Michael and Catherine and donor.*
Volterra, S. Girolamo. *Signed and dated 1466.*

843. BENVENUTO DI GIOVANNI: *Predella panel: Birth of the Virgin.* Volterra, Pinacoteca. *147(0?).*

844. BENVENUTO DI GIOVANNI: *Annunciation*. Detail. Sinalunga, S. Bernardino. *Signed and dated 1470.*

845. BENVENUTO DI GIOVANNI: *Predella panel: Expulsion of Adam and Eve*. Boston, Museum of Fine Arts.

846. BENVENUTO DI GIOVANNI: *Predella panel: Dead Christ upheld by Angels*. Florence, Berenson Collection.

847. BENVENUTO DI GIOVANNI: *Predella panel: S. James rescues the pilgrim.* Formerly Capesthorne Hall, Sir William Bromley Davenport.

848. BENVENUTO DI GIOVANNI: *Predella panel: Stoning of S. Stephen.* Homeless.

849–50. BENVENUTO DI GIOVANNI: *Stained glass window on his design: S. Michael, S. Catherine.*
Grosseto, Duomo.

851. BENVENUTO DI GIOVANNI: *S. Catherine of Siena bringing Pope Gregory back from Avignon.*
Detail of lunette. Siena, Società Esecutori Pie Disposizioni. *1501–2.*

852. Benvenuto di Giovanni: *Assumption with S. Thomas receiving the girdle between S. Francis and S. Anthony of Padua.* New York, Metropolitan Museum. *Signed and dated 1498.*

853. GIROLAMO DI BENVENUTO: *Assumption with S. Thomas receiving the girdle between S. Francis and S. Anthony of Padua.* Montalcino, Museo Diocesano. (*1498?*).

854–5. Girolamo di Benvenuto: *Two predella panels with Legend of Madonna of the Snow: Vision of the Roman Patrician*. Florence, Berenson Collection.—*Vision of Pope Liberius*. Homeless. *1508*.

856. GIROLAMO DI BENVENUTO: *Madonna and Child enthroned with SS. Dominic, Jerome, Catherine of Alexandria and Catherine of Siena, and Angels carrying snowballs.* Siena, Pinacoteca. *Signed and dated 1508.*

857. GIROLAMO DI BENVENUTO: *Predella panel: S. Catherine of Siena exorcizing a woman possessed by the Devil.* Denver, Colo., Museum of Art, Kress Collection.

858. Girolamo di Benvenuto: *Marriage salver: The Choice of Hercules*. Venice, Ca' d'Oro. *Early work.*

859. GIROLAMO DI BENVENUTO: *Marriage salver: Judgement of Paris.* Paris, Louvre. *Late work.*

860. GIROLAMO DI BENVENUTO: *Cleopatra.* Formerly Siena, Palazzo Chigi Saracini. *Late work.*

861. LIBERALE DA VERONA: *Miniature: Parable of the beam and the mote*. Siena, Duomo,
Libreria Piccolomini, Codex 9, fol. 1r.

863. LIBERALE DA VERONA: *Miniature: Parable of the Labourers in the Vineyard.* Siena, Duomo, Libreria Piccolomini, Codex 5, fol. 1r. Signed. Finished 1470.

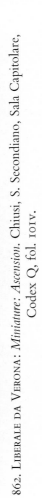

862. LIBERALE DA VERONA: *Miniature: Ascension.* Chiusi, S. Secondiano, Sala Capitolare, Codex Q, fol. 10v.

865. LIBERALE DA VERONA: *Madonna and Child with SS. Jerome and Anthony of Padua and four Angels.* Homeless.

864. LIBERALE DA VERONA: *Madonna and Child.* Formerly Budapest, Peteri Collection. *Early work.*

866. Liberale da Verona or Girolamo da Cremona: *Madonna and Child with SS. Benedict and Francesca Romana and Angels.* Rome, S. Francesca Romana. *1474.*

867. Liberale da Verona or Girolamo da Cremona: *Predella panel: S. Peter refuses Poppaea's alms.* Cambridge, Fitzwilliam Museum.

868. LIBERALE DA VERONA OR GIROLAMO DA CREMONA: *Blessing Christ with SS. John Evangelist, Leonard, Benedict, John Baptist and Bishop Settala as donor*. Viterbo, Duomo. *Dated 1472*.

tagantibus meritis ior
nostre salutis auxilium
prouenire concede. per

interceffione nos nsue.
cuius follennia celebra
mus. per onim nostrum.

869. GIROLAMO DA CREMONA: *Miniature: Nativity*. Mantua, Biblioteca. *1462–6*.

870. GIROLAMO DA CREMONA: *Miniature: S. Catherine before Maxentius*. London, Victoria and Albert Museum. *Signed*.

871. GIROLAMO DA CREMONA: *Miniature: Crucifixion*. Formerly Berlin, Schweizer Collection.

872. GIROLAMO DA CREMONA: *Miniature: Birth of the Virgin*. Siena, Duomo,
Libreria Piccolomini, Codex 12, fol. 64. *1472.*

873. GIROLAMO DA CREMONA: *Miniature: Birth of the Virgin*. Florence, Bargello, Breviario 68, fol. 125r.
1473–4.

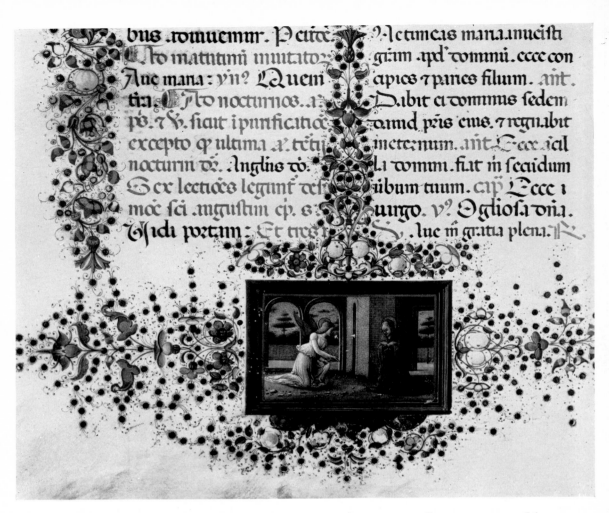

874. GIROLAMO DA CREMONA: *Miniature: Annunciation*. Florence, Bargello, Breviario 68, fol. 116v.
1473–4.

875. GIROLAMO DA CREMONA: *Annunciation*. Siena, Pinacoteca.

876. Francesco di Giorgio: *Miniature: Nativity*. Chiusi, S. Secondiano,
Antiphonary B, fol. 3. *About 1458–61*.

877. Girolamo da Cremona: *Miniature:*
Adoration of the Shepherds. Siena, Duomo,
Libreria Piccolomini, Codex 29, fol. 70. *1473*.

878. Girolamo da Cremona (on Liberale's design):
Miniature: Nativity. Siena, Duomo,
Libreria Piccolomini, Codex 29, fol. 58r. *1473*.

879-882. Francesco di Giorgio: *Illuminated page: Allegory of Chastity and three Labours of Hercules.*
Siena, Osservanza, Museo, Codex 3, fol. 1. *1463.*

883. Francesco di Giorgio: *Coronation*. Siena, Pinacoteca. *1471–2*.

884. Francesco di Giorgio: *Detached fresco: Fidelitas*. Los Angeles, Norton Simon Foundation.

885. FRANCESCO DI GIORGIO: *Cassone panel: Love bound*. Detail. Malibu, Cal., J. Paul Getty Museum.

886–7. NEROCCIO DI LANDI: *Spalliera panels: Putti in landscape*. Homeless.

888. FRANCESCO DI GIORGIO: *Wooden statue: S. John Baptist*. Detail. Fogliano, Parish Church.

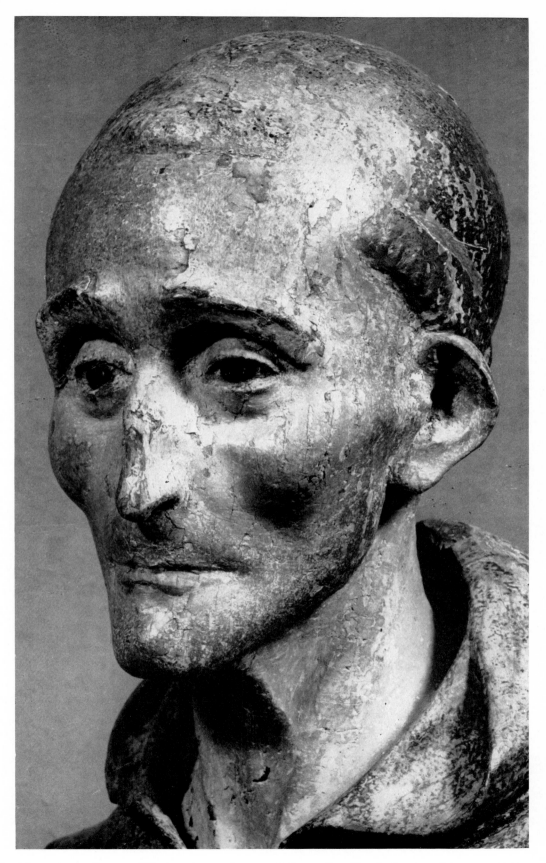

889. Neroccio di Landi: *Wooden pigmented statue: S. Bernardino*. Detail. Borgo a Mozzano, S. Jacopo.

891. Neroccio di Landi: *Book-cover: Madonna protecting Siena.*
Siena, Archivio di Stato. *Dated 1480.*

890. Francesco di Giorgio: *Book-cover: Madonna of the Earthquake.*
Siena, Archivio di Stato. *Dated 1467.*

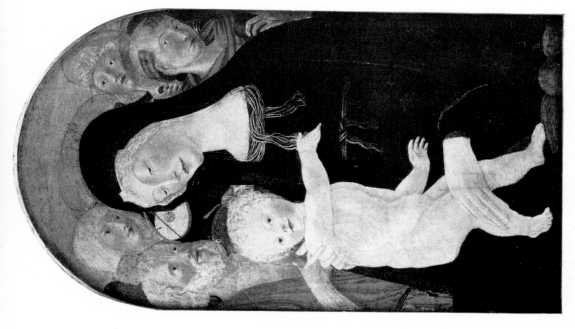

893. NEROCCIO DI LANDI: *Madonna and Child with SS. Jerome and Anthony of Padua and two Angels.* Florence, Berenson Collection.

892. FRANCESCO DI GIORGIO: *Madonna and Child with SS. Jerome and Bernardino.* Formerly Port Washington, S. R. Guggenheim.

894. NEROCCIO DI LANDI: *Tobias and the Angel*. Formerly Paris, Martin Le Roy.

895. Neroccio di Landi: *Lunette: Annunciation*. New Haven, Conn., Yale University Art Gallery. *About 1470.*

896. Neroccio di Landi: *Predella panel to Neroccio's Coronation for Monte Oliveto: Totila's visit to S. Benedict.* Florence, Uffizi. *1471–2?*

In the inscription on the pedestal:

IN CIBVM FEL INSITIM ACE
TVM DEDERVNT HANC
IN HOSPITALITATIS MOSTR
ABVNT MENSAM·TEMPLI
VERO SCINDETVR VELVM,
ET MEDIO DIE NOX ERIT
TENEBROSA TRIBVS HORIS

At the base:

SIBYLLA HELLESPONTICA IN A
GRO TROIANO NATA QVA SCRIBIT
HERACLIDES CYRI TEPORE FVISSE

897. NEROCCIO DI LANDI: *Marble intarsia on his design: Hellespontine Sibyl.* Siena, S. Maria Assunta. *1483.*

898. Neroccio di Landi: *Marble statue: S. Catherine of Siena*. Siena, Duomo. *1487–97*.

899. NEROCCIO DI LANDI: *Madonna and Child with SS. John Baptist and Catherine*. Los Angeles, County Museum.

900. NEROCCIO DI LANDI: *Madonna and Child with SS. Jerome and John Baptist*. Gazzada, Fondazione Cagnola.

901–2. NEROCCIO DI LANDI: *Two predella panels: Mystic Marriage of S. Catherine*. Formerly London, R. W. Christensen.—*S. Catherine's Vision of SS. Dominic, Francis and Bonaventura*. Florence, Berenson Collection.

903. NEROCCIO DI LANDI: *Madonna and Child with SS. Peter, Sigismund, Ansanus and Paul; in lunette, the Eternal and Cherubim*. Montisi, Pieve dell'Annunziata. *Signed and dated 1496.*

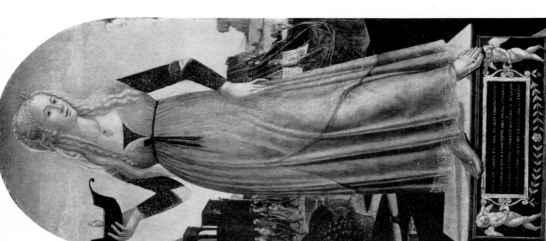

906. FRANCESCO DI GIORGIO (WITH MASTER OF GRISELDA): *Scipio Africanus.* Florence, Bargello.

905. NEROCCIO DI LANDI (WITH MASTER OF GRISELDA): *Vestal Claudia Quinta.* Washington, National Gallery of Art, Mellon Collection.

904. MASTER OF GRISELDA (WITH SIGNORELLI): *Alexander the Great.* Birmingham, Barber Institute.

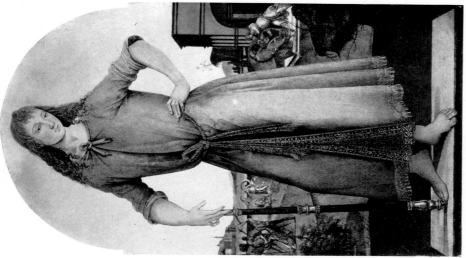

907. MASTER OF GRISELDA (WITH SIGNORELLI):
Tiberius Gracchus. Budapest, Museum of Fine Arts.

908. PACCHIAROTTO: *Sulpicia.*
Baltimore, Walters Art Gallery.

909. MASTER OF GRISELDA (WITH SIGNORELLI):
Eunustus of Tanagra (cut at bottom). Washington,
National Gallery of Art, Kress Collection.

910. MASTER OF GRISELDA: *Detail of cassone panel: The Story of the patient Griselda—The Marriage*. London, National Gallery.

911. MASTER OF GRISELDA: *Scene from Roman History*. Detail. Longleat, Marquess of Bath.

912. MASTER OF GRISELDA: *Cassone panel: Story of the patient Griselda—The Restoration*. Detail.
London, National Gallery.

913. Pietro di Domenico da Siena (on Francesco di Giorgio's cartoon): *Disrobing of Christ.*
Siena, Pinacoteca.

914. Pietro di Domenico da Siena: *Assumption; below, Nativity and six Saints*. Radicondoli, Collegiata.

916. PIETRO DI DOMENICO DA SIENA: *Adoration of the Shepherds,
with Procession of the Magi in the background. Siena, Pinacoteca.*

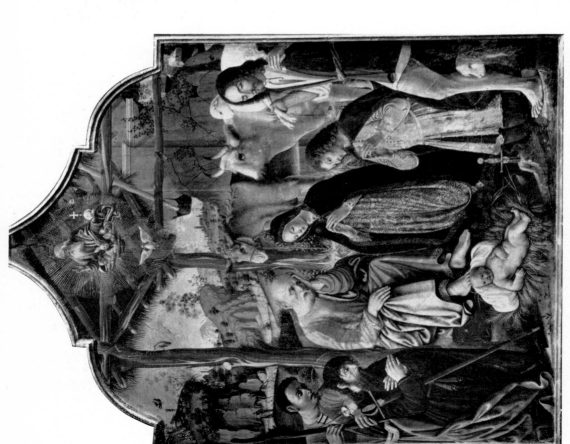

915. PIETRO DI DOMENICO DA SIENA: *Nativity with SS. Galganus and Martin.
Siena, Pinacoteca. Signed.*

918. PACCHIAROTTO: *Nativity with SS. Bernardino and Anthony of Padua.*
Formerly Massa Marittima, S. Agostino. *Early work.*

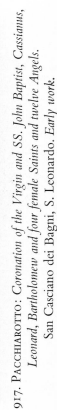

917. PACCHIAROTTO: *Coronation of the Virgin and SS. John Baptist, Cassianus,*
Leonard, Bartholomew and four female Saints and twelve Angels.
San Casciano dei Bagni, S. Leonardo. *Early work.*

919. PACCHIAROTTO: *Madonna and Child with
SS. John Baptist and Jerome.* Formerly Siena,
Barzelotti Camaiori Collection.

920. PACCHIAROTTO: *Madonna and Child with
SS. Jerome and Anthony of Padua.* Homeless.
Late work.

921. PACCHIAROTTO: *Madonna and Child with SS. Onophrius and Bartholomew and Angels.* Siena, Pinacoteca.

922. PACCHIAROTTO: *Visitation with SS. John Baptist, Anthony Abbot, Anthony of Padua, Nicholas, Dominic and Leonard*. Siena, Pinacoteca. *About 1530.*

923. PACCHIAROTTO: *Holy Family and four Angels*. Detail. La Gaida, Gino Magnani Collection.

924–5. PACCHIAROTTO: *Two predella panels: Baptism; Resurrection*. Cambridge, Fitzwilliam Museum.

926. PACCHIAROTTO: *Ascension*. Siena, Pinacoteca.

927. FUNGAI: *Coronation of the Virgin with Saints and Angels.* Formerly Amsterdam, Otto Lanz.

928. FUNGAI: *Madonna and Child.* Homeless.

929. FUNGAI: *Madonna adoring the Child, with two Angels.* Formerly New York, Percy S. Straus.

930. FUNGAI: *S. Catherine receiving stigmata*. Siena, Santuario Cateriniano, Oratorio della Cucina. *1497*.

OPVS · BENNĀDINI   FVNGHARII·DESENIS

931. FUNGAI: *Dead Christ upheld by two Angels*. Formerly Siena, Monistero di S. Eugenio.

932. FUNGAI: *Predella panel: S. Clement striking water from the rock*. York, City Art Gallery.

933. FUNGAI: *Nativity with SS. Vincent and Jerome; in predella, Martyrdom and Beheading of S. Vincent, Adoration of the Magi, S. Jerome and the lion, S. Jerome in the wilderness; in pilasters, Angel and Virgin of the Annunciation, SS. Stephen, Sebastian, Catherine of Alexandria and Catherine of Siena. Chiusi, S. Secondiano.*

934. FUNGAI: *Cassone panel: Scipio and the thieves*. Formerly London, W. H. Woodward.

935. FUNGAI: *Cassone panel: Rescue of Hippo*. Left half. Houston, Texas, Museum of Art.

936. FUNGAI: *Cassone panel: Scipio goes to the Capitol.* Formerly London, W. H. Woodward.

937. FUNGAI: *Cassone panel: Rescue of Hippo.* Right half. Houston, Texas, Museum of Art.

938. FUNGAI: *Madonna and Child enthroned*. Detail.
Montenero, Chiesa della Madonna.

939. FUNGAI: *Predella panel: Communion of S. Mary Magdalen with Noli me tangere in the background.*
Siena, S. Domenico.

940. FUNGAI: *Coronation of the Virgin with SS. Jerome, Sebastian, Anthony of Padua and Nicholas.*
Siena, Pinacoteca. *Signed and dated 1512.*

BARTOLOMMEO DELLA GATTA, LUCA SIGNORELLI AND THE RETARDATAIRE UMBRO-MARCHIGIANS OF THE XV-XVI CENTURY

941. Bartolommeo della Gatta: *View of Arezzo.*
Detail from *S. Roch imploring Christ to save Arezzo from the Plague.*
Arezzo, Pinacoteca.

942. Bartolommeo della Gatta: *S. Roch imploring the Virgin.*
Arezzo, Pinacoteca. *Dated 1479.*

943. BARTOLOMMEO DELLA GATTA: *Madonna and Child enthroned with SS. Julian, Peter, Paul and Michael.*
Castiglion Fiorentino, Collegiata di S. Giuliano. *1486.*

944. BARTOLOMMEO DELLA GATTA: *S. Francis receiving stigmata.*
Castiglion Fiorentino, Pinacoteca. *1487.*

945. BARTOLOMMEO DELLA GATTA: *Predella panel: Story of S. Julian.* Castiglion Fiorentino,
Collegiata di S. Giuliano. *1486.*

946. BARTOLOMMEO DELLA GATTA: *Detail from the Assumption*. Cortona, S. Domenico.

947. SIGNORELLI: *Flagellation*. Milan, Brera. *Signed. Early work.*

948. SIGNORELLI: *Madonna and Child enthroned with SS. Onuphrius, John Baptist, Lawrence and Herculanus (or Bishop Jacopo Vannucci). Perugia, Opera del Duomo. Formerly dated 1484.*

949. SIGNORELLI: *Male portrait*. Berlin-Dahlem, Staatliche Museen. *Early work.*

950. SIGNORELLI: *Fragment of a Deposition*. Capesthorne Hall, Mrs. Bromley Davenport.

951. SIGNORELLI: *Detail from Christ on the Cross*. Florence, Uffizi.

952. SIGNORELLI: *Mourning women. Detail from Christ on the Cross*. Florence, Uffizi.

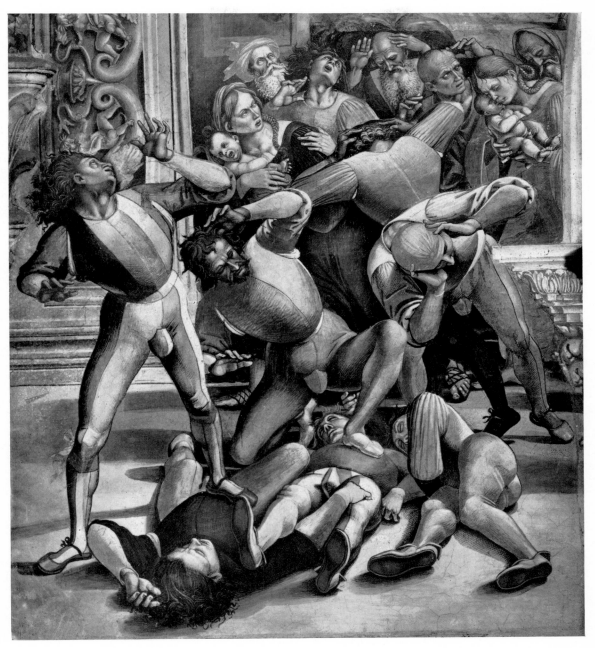

953. SIGNORELLI: *The End of the World. Detail of fresco.* Orvieto, Duomo. *1499–503.*

954. SIGNORELLI: *Resurrection*. Homeless.

955. SIGNORELLI: *Predella panel: SS. John Baptist and Jerome appearing to S. Augustine.*
London, National Gallery. *1519.*

956. SIGNORELLI AND ASSISTANTS: *Altarpiece: Baptism of Christ; in predella, Birth of S. John Baptist,*
S. John Baptist preaching, Reproach of Herod and Herodias, Dance of Salome, Beheading of S. John Baptist.
(Saints in pilasters by Francesco di Gentile da Fabriano; Angel and Virgin of the Annunciation
by Antonio da Fabriano?) Arcevia, S. Medardo. *1508.*

958. LORENZO D'ALESSANDRO: *Detail of triptych: Madonna and Child, S. Mary Magdalen.*
Corridonia, Pinacoteca. *Signed and dated 1481.*

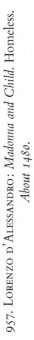

957. LORENZO D'ALESSANDRO: *Madonna and Child.* Homeless.
About 1480.

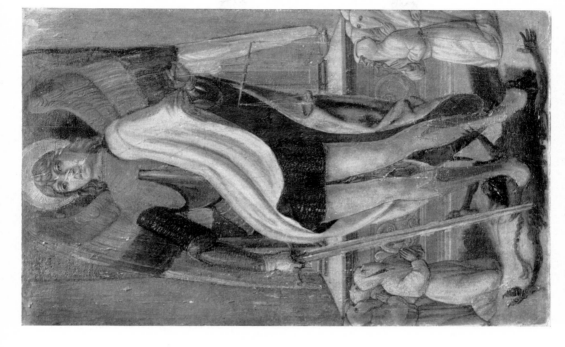

960. LORENZO D'ALESSANDRO: *Processional standard: S. Michael worshipped by Flagellants.* Baltimore, Walters Art Gallery.

959. LORENZO D'ALESSANDRO: *Madonna holding a ribbon which encircles two tables supported by Saints.* Caldarola, S. Maria del Monte. *Signed and dated 1491.*

961. LORENZO D'ALESSANDRO: *Detail of frescoed niche: S. John Baptist and donor.* Sarnano, S. Maria di Piazza. *Signed and dated 1483.*

962. LORENZO D'ALESSANDRO: *S. Anthony of Padua worshipping the Virgin.* Pollenza, SS. Francesco e Antonio da Padova. *Signed and dated 1496.*

963. LORENZO D'ALESSANDRO: *Polyptych: Madonna and Child, SS. James, Peter, Francis and Sebastian; above, Dead Christ upheld by Angels, SS. Catherine, Michael, John Baptist and Bonaventure; in predella, twelve Apostles, and SS. Catherine, Apollonia, Nicholas and Lucy*. Serrapetrona, Parish Church. *Formerly dated 1494*.

964. MASTER OF THE CRIVELLESQUE POLYPTYCHS: *Reconstruction of polyptych from Tocco Casauria: S. Anthony of Padua with S. Bonaventura in pinnacle; Madonna adoring the Child in her lap, Dead Christ with Symbols of the Passion in pinnacle. Aquila, Museo Nazionale.— S. Francis with S. Louis of Toulouse in pinnacle. Assisi, Basilica, Museo.—S. John Baptist with S. Bernardino in pinnacle; S. Jerome with S. John of Capistrano in pinnacle. Chieti, Museo Civico. 1489.*

965. MASTER OF THE CRIVELLESQUE POLYPTYCHS: *Polyptych: Madonna adoring the Child in her lap; SS. Bonaventura, Michael, Francis and Bernardino of Siena; in pinnacles, Dead Christ with Symbols of the Passion and SS. Clare, Louis of France, Louis of Toulouse and John of Capistrano; in predella, the twelve Apostles. Formerly Harewood House, Earl of Harewood.*

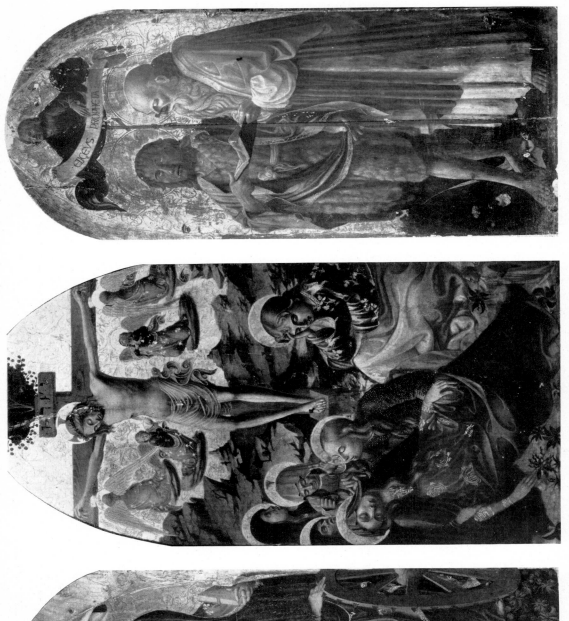

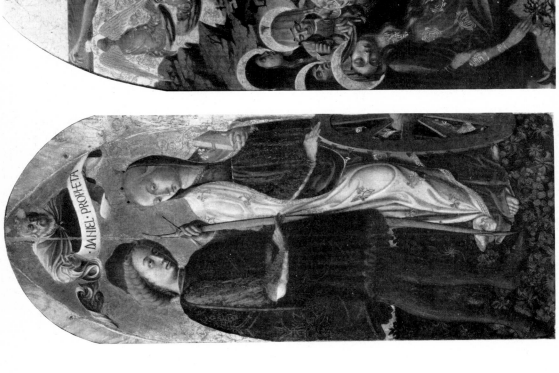

966–8. URBANI: *Two side-panels and pinnacle of polyptych: SS. Sebastian and Catherine with the Prophet Daniel above; SS. John Baptist and Romuald with the Prophet Elisha above.* Matelica, S. Teresa.—*Crucifixion.* Colmar, Musée Unterlinden.

970. URBANI: *Madonna and Child enthroned with SS. Anthony Abbot and Nicholas.*
Formerly Recanati, S. Maria di Castelnuovo. *Signed and dated 1480.*

969. URBANI(?): *Assumption of S. Mary Magdalen.* Homeless.

971. FRANCESCO DI GENTILE DA FABRIANO: *Triptych: Madonna and Child enthroned with Angels, S. Francis, S. Bernardino*. Matelica, S. Francesco.

972. FRANCESCO DI GENTILE DA FABRIANO: *Predella panel: Crucifixion*. Formerly Derby, A. W. Pugin. *1462*.

973. FRANCESCO DI GENTILE DA FABRIANO:
Centre panel of polyptych: Madonna and Child enthroned with Angels.
Formerly Derby, A. W. Pugin. *1462.*

974–5. Francesco di Gentile da Fabriano: *Side-panels of polyptych: SS. Jerome and Giovanni di Prato; SS. Clement and Sebastian.* Formerly Derby, A. W. Pugin. *1462.*

976–8. Francesco di Gentile da Fabriano:
Two Angels. Rome, Galleria Nazionale.—*S. Bernardino.* Homeless.

979–80. Francesco di Gentile da Fabriano: *Processional standard: S. Sebastian with SS. Anthony Abbot and Dominic, and Baptist in pinnacle; Madonna in glory, and blessing Christ in pinnacle.* Milan, Brera.

981. Francesco di Gentile da Fabriano: *Ecce homo.* Washington, Dumbarton Oaks. *Signed.*   982. Francesco di Gentile da Fabriano: *Ecce homo.* Formerly Melchett Court, Lord Melchett.

983. GIOVANNI PAGANI DA MONTERUBBIANO: *Madonna del Soccorso*. Montpellier, Musée Fabre.
Signed and dated 1506.

984. BERNARDINO DI MARIOTTO: *Madonna del Soccorso*. San Severino Marche, Duomo Nuovo.
Signed and dated 1509.

985. Bernardino di Mariotto: *Mystic Marriage of S. Catherine, with SS. Peter, Mary Magdalen, Bishop Saint and Infant S. John Baptist*. Perugia, Galleria Nazionale dell'Umbria.

986. BERNARDINO DI MARIOTTO: *Madonna and Child in glory with SS. Severinus, Catherine of Siena, Dominic, Florentius and Infant S. John.* San Severino Marche, S. Domenico. *1512–14.*

987. BERNARDINO DA MARIOTTO: *Predella panel: Communion of S. Colomba da Rieti.* Homeless.

988. BERNARDINO DI MARIOTTO: *Predella panel: Christ disputing with the Doctors.* Rome, Principe Colonna.

989. BERNARDINO DI MARIOTTO: *Madonna and Child with SS. Anne, Roch, Sebastian and Angels*. Detail. Perugia, Galleria Nazionale dell'Umbria.

990. BERNARDINO DI MARIOTTO: *Predella panel: Circumcision*. Formerly Richmond, Cook Collection.

991. VINCENZO PAGANI: *Madonna and Child with SS. Peter and Francis and two music-making Angels.*
Corridonia, S. Francesco. *Signed and dated 1517.*

992. VINCENZO PAGANI: *Predella panel: Christ disputing with the Doctors.* Milan, Brera.

993. VINCENZO PAGANI: *Coronation of the Virgin with SS. Genesio(?), John Evangelist, Bonaventura and Ursula.*
Milan, Brera. *1517–18.*

994. VINCENZO PAGANI: *Deposition*. Sarnano, Pinacoteca. *Signed and dated 1529.*